YOU DESERVE THIS SH!T

Get Unstuck, Find Your Path, and
Become the Best Version of Yourself

JORDAN TARVER

www.jordantarver.com

Copyright © 2021 Jordan Tarver.

All rights reserved. No part of this book may be reproduced, stored, or transmitted by any means—whether auditory, graphic, mechanical, or electronic—without written permission of both publisher and author, except in the case of brief excerpts used in critical articles and reviews. Unauthorized reproduction of any part of this work is illegal and is punishable by law.

This book is for you.

CONTENTS

Your Journey Starts Here   1
Setting the Stage   7

PART I: AWARENESS

Chapter 1: What You'll Learn About Awareness   23
Chapter 2: Your First Step Is Most Crucial   26
Chapter 3: Notice Everything, Even the Small Things   38
Chapter 4: Honest Self-Questioning   42
Chapter 5: Adapt to Your Surroundings   49
Chapter 6: When In Doubt, Close Your Eyes   58
Chapter 7: Awareness: What You Can Do With These Lessons   67

PART II: COMFORT ZONES

Chapter 8: What You'll Learn About Comfort Zones   73
Chapter 9: Build Trust With Yourself   77
Chapter 10: Reject the Normal   84
Chapter 11: Give Yourself Permission to Be a Beginner   92

Chapter 12: Curiosity of Experience	99
Chapter 13: Complacency: A True Sickness	107
Chapter 14: Growth Hacking Failure	117
Chapter 15: Separate Yourself From Familiarity	124
Chapter 16: Comfort Zones: What You Can Do With These Lessons	130

PART III: INTENTIONAL LIVING

Chapter 17: What You'll Learn About Intentional Living	139
Chapter 18: The Power of Routine	142
Chapter 19: Thoughts Are Energy	151
Chapter 20: Cultivate Valuable Relationships	160
Chapter 21: Choose Your Atmosphere	170
Chapter 22: Build Your System	182
Chapter 23: Your Life Will Be As Big As Your Aspirations	191
Chapter 24: Intentional Living: What You Can Do With These Lessons	198
Chapter 25: This Book Is Your Nudge	204
Free Bonus Content	211
Acknowledgements	213
About the Author	219

YOUR JOURNEY STARTS HERE

"There is a candle in your heart, ready to be kindled.
There is a void in your soul, ready to be filled.
You feel it, don't you?"

— Rumi

Self-discovery is not a journey to discover someone new, it's a journey to break down the barriers within yourself to discover who your soul always knew you were. The journey you're about to embark on will guide you toward kindling the candle in your heart and filling the void in your soul. Are you ready to take action?

Before we get down to business, it's crucial to define what self-discovery actually means, and what would happen if you avoided taking the journey. Self-discovery is a process of understanding your own character and becoming aware of your potential and motives. If you discover yourself, you're able to tap into your passions, figure out your life's purpose—the reason you get up in the morning—and learn what motivates you. Ultimately, discovering who you are and what you want to do allows you to unlock the best version of yourself.

Without discovering yourself—understanding your purpose, passions, potential, and motives—you'll never achieve something better than what you have now. You'll choose to live a life inundated by unconsciousness and the pain that comes along with it.

The purpose of this book is to teach you the three pillars of self-discovery—awareness, comfort zones, and intentional living—you'll need these tools for your journey. Learning about these pillars will help you discover who you are and aid you in the process of becoming the best version of yourself. When you discover who you are, you'll be set free of taking the wrong paths in life.

Now you may be thinking, *What if I feel like I've already discovered who I was always meant to be?* That's okay. You see, this book isn't only about uncovering your path; it is also about living a more meaningful life. This book will help you discover ways to reinvent yourself or come more fully into yourself, and within these pages, I share the lessons that gave me the opportunity to evolve into my true, authentic self.

This book is a testament to how your actions and decisions can define your path. But these aren't all the answers. Nobody can give you all the answers because each person is unique, with their own individual passions, their own purpose, and their own reason for being. Although I don't have all the answers for you in this book, the ones I have may change your life. I learned these lessons through personal experiences with different cultures, tests of patience, overcoming frustration, and solving the puzzles life threw at me. This book is the result of tireless work focused on creative self-growth.

Think about what brought you to this book and why you were called to open these pages. What are you searching for?

There's a possibility you're sitting at home right now smiling at everything that surrounds you—happiness, money, certainty, success, confidence, and a perfect understanding of who you are. You have just about everything figured out, and you're not sure if there's anything else you can do to unlock your greatest potential. Because, well, you've already done that and it's laughable to even think you're not functioning at your highest vibration. You happen to be an enlightened one—you have your shit figured out. Life was once difficult for you, but you've cracked the code. You've found what it takes to accomplish life in the most, let's say, beautiful and seemingly perfect way. However, people like that are few and far between. In fact, in my eyes, they don't exist. There's always work to do.

Maybe you already know how important it is to follow your heart and follow your gut but don't have the awareness to recognize or interpret the feelings associated with those promptings. You run through life quickly and forget to slow down and focus on yourself—you neglect to take the proper time to hear your call and chase it. This book will teach you how to become more aware, and more self-aware, which will help open the doors to what's within you. Being self-aware helps you understand what makes you happy and gets you in touch with your surroundings. Awareness offers clarity on how to adapt to the world around you and provides insight into the depth of your life beyond materialism. If this is you—someone who knows they need to follow their gut but hasn't yet sensed what's within—*this book is for you.*

There's a chance you're also this: you think you thrive off living comfortably, but you've started to realize that living within your comfort zone doesn't present you with challenges that will guide you to the best version of yourself. You're ready to jump ship and push your chips all in on chasing something different. This is a time where you are standing face to face with the opportunity to be unique and doing something others may find "weird." But don't discount your weirdness—it's what will lead you to be your most authentic self and let you stand out as a person. Embrace it. Do what you want to do, not what others tell you to do. Give yourself permission to let go. If this is you—someone who is ready to live outside their comfort zone and really start their life—*this book is for you.*

Do you have trouble leading an intentional life? Do you float around not paying close attention to your habits and goals, or fail to think of a system to accomplish those endeavors? Maybe you've never heard of intentional living until now, so you're sitting there thinking, *Oh shit, that's me.* Good, because you've opened the right book. This book is a masterclass that will teach you the necessary lessons to become more conscious of your daily life and the manner in which you live. It's time to focus on what matters and approach life with intention. If this is you—someone who mindlessly makes decisions, hasn't built a robust system to accomplish their goals, and doesn't put conscious effort into choosing who and what you surround yourself with—*this book is for you.*

Here's the thing: If you are struggling to discover your path and purpose, you have a spot on the roster. Maybe you've never tried to uncover what moves you physically and emotionally, or maybe you've always been in the shadows of those who came before you. There's also a possibility your inner voice has taken over and is in complete control of the trajectory of your life's arc. Regardless of the roadblocks and hiccups you've experienced in life so far, if you are here, it's clear you're ready to take the first step into something bigger than yourself—uncovering the best version of yourself.

I've lived through all of those situations. I lacked confidence, I was afraid to do anything unique or challenging, I wasn't comfortable with being uncomfortable, and I was *not* living my truth or being my most authentic self. I knew I needed to shift things in my life—my thoughts, my mindset, my energy, the way I talked to myself. I've been there. I've experienced lows, but I was able to follow the light and emerge from the tunnel. So can you.

No matter where you are in life right now, you're capable of making changes to improve the rest of your journey. Every moment is an opportunity to turn things around. Grasp that understanding and run free.

Something about this book called you. Something in your life made you feel like you were meant to pick up this book and read. That feeling—your intuition—rests in your gut. Intuition is a sense we all feel innately, yet it's something no one can truly explain. It can serve as your voice of reason, or a leading piece of guidance to lean on. I'm glad you followed the feeling to pick up this book, because I believe you deserve this shit.

Welcome to a piece of work that offers lessons you can incorporate into your daily life. Some may resonate, others may not. Adopt the lessons that connect with your vibration and use them to better yourself.

Let's get this show on the road.

SETTING THE STAGE

My journey has never been easy, but that's honestly true for a lot of people. Life is hard, let's recognize that before diving into this masterclass. Before we get started, I want to share a secret that may change the way you think forever: You will never discover your path and purpose until you begin to invent it.

In this chapter, a few things are going to happen. We will first learn what it truly means to become the best version of yourself. Right now that may not mean much to you, but I want it to mean everything. I want it to be your guiding light moving forward, and I want you to feel as if becoming the best version of yourself is your life's greatest calling—it's one of mine.

Once you grasp that understanding, it's likely your vision and energy will shift for the remainder of your life. The choices you make and the manner in which you act will revolve around being the most authentic, best version of yourself.

We will also discuss a little bit about who I was and who I am now. There was a turning point in my life when the thought *I'm going to do something outside my comfort zone* became a decision that completely changed the trajectory of my life's arc. There was "me" before that decision, and there was a completely new, redefined version—the best version—of "me" after that decision.

Creating my own identity is a manifestation of my entire life, and it will continue to manifest. My identity has its roots in my childhood—how I was raised, how I felt in social situations, and, ultimately, how I felt internally about myself. This is meant to shine light on the potential you have, too, regardless of your past.

Finally, this chapter is also here to help explain how to use this book and the goal of the book. This chapter will show you the value you'll be able to take from the book and implement immediately.

This book is built on three pillars: awareness, comfort zones, and intentional living. Through my own journey of self-discovery, I've come to believe that these three pillars are the foundation of becoming the best version of yourself and unlocking your greatest potential. While these pillars may seem insignificant, the smallest aspects of life can be the most powerful.

WHAT'S THE BEST VERSION OF YOURSELF, AND WHY SHOULD YOU CARE?

What does it mean to become the best version of yourself? Who is that person and why does it even matter? These are the questions I've asked myself over the years, not only to understand my journey but to come up with answers for you.

Before we dig into this section, we need to get a few things straight that will help you understand what the best version of yourself is and why it matters. Purpose, passion, and potential are words that get tossed around a lot, and they're possibly used interchangeably due to a lack of understanding. These three words are the focal point not only of my life but several others', too.

It's important to understand the true meaning of purpose, passion, and potential because in truth, they're *not* interchangeable. However, they can build on each other. Let's first learn of their meanings and then piece together how they can relate to each other:

- **Purpose:** Your purpose is *not* your title or occupation. Your purpose is the reason you get out of bed every morning, the reason you chase your different endeavors. Your purpose is your offering to the world.

    My purpose is not my professional job. Rather, my purpose is to live a creative and adventurous life and encourage others to be the best versions of themselves. That's why I believe I'm here, to deliver that message through my passions.

- **Passion:** Your passion is *not* your purpose. Your passions are the activities—your callings—that give you life. Your passion is the medium through which you can reveal your purpose. It's an endeavor that gives you the opportunity to deliver your message—your offering to the world.

My passion is creativity—writing, photography, music, inspiring others—which gives me the opportunity to deliver my message, my offering, *my purpose* to the world. Without this passion, I wouldn't be able to inspire others to do great things and become the best version of themselves.

- **Potential:** Your potential is *not* your purpose or passion. Your potential is the capacity of success and growth you give yourself permission to achieve. It's not dictated by anyone else but yourself. Your potential is a decision, it's your decision.

    My potential, and your potential, is what we tell ourselves we can achieve. Everyone has an equal opportunity to experience the greatest potential; however, not everyone has the same outcome because of the self-limiting beliefs they impose on themselves.

Connecting your purpose, passion, and potential can help you become the best version of yourself. Your purpose, passion, and potential make up *who you are*, *what you do*, and *why you do it*. So, without further ado, this is how the three connect (and a *very* important equation in all of our lives):

*Your **potential** is the permission you give yourself to achieve success through your **passion** while being able to spread your **purpose** through offering value to the world.*

The best version of yourself is the person that encompasses just that. It's the version of you that marries your purpose, passion, and potential in a genuine way that allows you to honor yourself. Living like this allows you to feel perfectly wired to achieve your greatest dreams. This lifestyle will give you the energy, confidence, and motivation to chase exactly what you want to chase. This way of living will make you feel in control of your life and give you the opportunity to gain clarity on what you need to do to feel fulfilled.

And why should you care? Because you have one opportunity to live the life you want. You deserve to become the person you were always meant to be and to flourish. Striving to become the best version of yourself doesn't need to become a pain point in your life. Let go of self-pressure and learn to live through joy and playfulness.

With this attitude, you'll slowly open up to receiving *your* answer. You'll begin to see that evolving into the best version of yourself can be one of the most exciting and rewarding aspects of life. Grasp onto that journey, it can take you to incredible places.

CREATING MY OWN IDENTITY

I grew up in a family of six—two older brothers, an older sister, and, of course, my loving parents. Raised in a small town in Sonoma County, I like to think my innocence was long-lasting, as there was never much influence outside my family, church, sports, and early years of schooling.

I attended a private school until I was about 12 years old, which consisted of one schoolhouse that maxed out at 40 students. The place was small—everyone knew everyone and their parents and their grandparents and where they lived and their home phone numbers.

Parents never have a true rule book to go by when raising their children. My parents taught themselves the ropes they believed would give their children a life worth living—a life where we could flourish beyond our own imagination.

My parents were good at a lot of things. In particular, they always created a space for us to follow our interests. There was never a predetermined path for us to follow. They gifted us with the power to make those types of decisions and sit in the driver's seat of our life. Although this may seem like a lack of guidance, it was far from that. It taught me that I was able to guide the trajectory of my life—I was able to invent my own identity.

However, in my early teens, I wasn't sure who I was, and I lacked self-confidence. They weren't my best years. I second-guessed who I was trying to be, felt like I didn't fit in with the people around me, and couldn't find my voice. Although I was uncertain and far from confident, I was able to rely on the foundation my parents built for me.

During my high school years, I realized that I felt a bit lost. But this motivated me. The feeling of being lost and unsure of myself encouraged me to redefine who I was and step into my own power.

After graduating from California State University, Fullerton, I had a piece of paper that said I had earned a bachelor's degree in business finance. A common path is to follow what you learned in college and make a career out of it. However, that didn't sit right with me. Finance wasn't *my thing*. It didn't bring me joy.

While it may be easy to believe you must follow what you "found" in college, those traditional ways of thinking are a thing of the past. I realized this and pledged to live a life solely built on the foundation of following my interests and heart. My heart led me to a different path. It showed me the gateway to my own self-discovery and encouraged me to seek something that resonated with me, rather than follow the traditional ways of thinking.

So, instead of beginning a journey dictated by the words on that piece of paper—business finance—I decided to take a leap of faith. I was ready to crack open the door to my own self-discovery and create my true identity. I was mature enough to understand that the past doesn't have to define your future, and I had the ability to make significant changes in my life.

I moved out of my house in Newport Beach that was just steps from the sand, quit my job as a restaurant server days after graduating college, packed a backpack full of clothes and essentials, and left for a three-month solo backpacking trip across Europe. I felt the need to maneuver myself through a very unfamiliar place. I began to see this as an intensive masterclass. The subject? My own life.

I challenged myself to leave a positive impact on every single individual I connected with, and I wrote down everything in my leather journal. Everything from where I was staying, to what city I was in, to the sketchy gypsy on the side of the road, to the times when I was about ready to cry, and then give up and fly home. Some days were tougher than others, but my anchor was remembering the greater purpose of the journey—the opportunity to become who I was always meant to be.

My other two anchors in my life at that point were the best efforts I put forth to try and positively impact the people I met and the hundred or so cream-colored pages in my leather journal.

For the first time in my life, I embraced writing. I was using my voice. Positivity and writing became my method of release—they let me express my most authentic self. Although I felt nervous to embrace this path because it was a new endeavor, I was confident of one thing: The voice that comes from the deepest part of our hearts and the feeling that burns in the center of our gut is usually the guide we need to learn to love and understand. And so I did.

I saw this path as a gateway, as an opportunity for self-realization and change. It was my chance to break through to the other side and create a life I would be proud to live.

Writing slowly became an addiction. Through it, I was able to learn so much about myself. I had a lot to reflect on in my collection of journal entries made over those three months.

To extract the lessons from that journey, I compiled my journal into a book titled *Moment, Vol. I: To Whom It May Concern*. While the majority of the book is filled with direct journal entries, I wrote present-day reflections to uncover the purpose of my journey of self-actualization. I was tirelessly trying to crack the code.

What was the real reason I did all of this? Why did I need to isolate myself to find myself? So many questions ran through my head, and each one of them had an incredibly valuable answer and lesson. I was motivated to investigate what those moments held—what else I could uncover and use to my advantage. Not only for me to learn, but for me to teach others, too. I began to uncover diamond after diamond. I was able to uncover the riches of my life by using self-reflection as my pickaxe. I discovered that I created my own identity.

If you want to create your identity and become the best version of yourself, then place yourself outside your comfort zone. While you're out there, embrace your childlike curiosity and don't underestimate the power of that curiosity. My curiosity led me to my most authentic identity and reason for being. You have the opportunity to discover yours, too. Plant your seed and let it grow.

HOW TO USE THIS BOOK

While a how-to book would be *really* nice, I don't quite think that's appropriate for the purpose of this book: discovering meaning in life through your journey of self-discovery.

No two journeys are the same; no two people have identical routes to self-discovery. To think they do, and to write a step-by-step guide on how to discover yourself would be a disservice on my part. I'm not here to guide you with fluffy information to make you think you can follow specific steps to unlock your maximum potential—the best version of yourself. That journey is in your hands. The decisions you make and the effort you put forth in your self-discovery is up to *you*.

However, with that being said, what I can teach you are the foundational qualities you should embrace if you want to live with more meaning and discover who you were always meant to be. This book embodies just that.

Through my own struggles, I discovered a handful of ideas, qualities, and tools that continue to help me every day in my own pursuit of living my best life. These discoveries are within these pages, and this book is separated into three parts. Each focus on one of the three pillars of self-discovery:

- **Part I:** Awareness
- **Part II:** Comfort Zones
- **Part III:** Intentional Living

In each part, you'll read about lessons I learned on my journey. These lessons will teach you aspects of life that are crucial to your own self-discovery journey and can help you become the best version of yourself.

It would be wrong to assume that the steps I took to find meaning in my life will be identical for you. I believe we can all use the same tools, but we each need to take steps that resonate with our individual selves. In other words, the route I took, and the route you take, may be completely different.

What matters is that we both strive to live a life infused with meaning that allows us to become the best versions of ourselves. The ideas in this toolkit can do this for you, as they did for me.

THE GOAL OF THIS BOOK

I understand time is valuable, but, more importantly, I understand *your* time is valuable. With that in mind, I didn't want to write a book about what I need. I wanted to write a book about something you need.

From the first time I sat down to write my shitty first draft until I put the finishing touches on the book during the final edit stage, you've always been the motivator for me to finish. Knowing that just one person might read this and gain a life-changing lesson was enough to keep the fuel burning.

Now, I've never felt like I owed you something or that I was indebted to you; however, I always felt like I owed it to myself to share these lessons and experiences.

The goal of this book is to provide a toolkit for your own self-discovery and becoming the best version of yourself. I've always believed it's important to share what you know, especially if it has changed your life, because of the likely chance it could do the same for many other people. We're all a community here, and we should be willing to teach others our life hacks, practices, exercises, lessons, and experiences with the idea that it could make another person's life more fulfilling. I'm here and writing this to do just that—to give you what I know because I want you to live the life you deserve.

This book is built on three pillars that are the foundation of becoming the best version of yourself. These are the tools

I believe we all need to unlock our greatest potential and live in a manner that allows us to deliver our purpose through our biggest passions. For me, the three pillars below are my highest priorities. I focus on them often and always strive to understand them more and more.

With the three pillars of self-discovery, you can start to build your journey, discover your path, and unlock your greatest potential. Learn what these pillars can do for your life and incorporate the lessons that resonate with you most, they may just be your savior:

1. **Awareness:** Understand your character, feelings, and what inspires you. Begin to realize and accept the things that move you physically, emotionally, and mentally. Nothing can change without awareness.
2. **Comfort Zones:** To create space for opportunity, we must exit our safe zones and challenge ourselves to stand for uniqueness. Everything in life begins to flourish outside our comfort zones. That's where the magic happens.
3. **Intentional Living:** Make conscious efforts to live aligned with your truest values and beliefs. Your decisions define you and choosing a life that matters is completely in your hands.

The three pillars of self-discovery—awareness, comfort zones, and intentional living—will be the catalyst to catapulting your journey or leveling up on your current path. Through the lessons within each pillar, you'll gain a new, refreshing understanding of things to place high value on in your own life. By embodying these three pillars, you'll be well on your way to unlocking your greatest potential and living the life you deserve.

However, before we get this party started, there's one thing we need to agree on: not everything in this book will resonate with you, and that's okay. We're all unique individuals. What may work for someone else, might not work for you. The quicker we understand that, the better the process will be.

There's also a chance that everything in this book resonates, and that's also okay. Don't use the number of lessons that resonate as a metric of where you are on your journey. Drop that thought and get excited for any lessons that vibe with your life. Hold them close and begin to find ways to implement them immediately.

The easiest way to create positive change is to take action. Find things about your life you never knew were there and capitalize on them. Double down and become completely tunnel vision as if your life depended on it, because it kind of does—especially if you crave making some amazing changes. I've committed to investing in myself. I've learned from the trials and tribulations of my own self-discovery. You're next.

PART I
AWARENESS

Understand your character, feelings, and what inspires you. Begin to realize and accept the things that move you physically, emotionally, and mentally. Nothing can change without awareness.

#1
WHAT YOU'LL LEARN ABOUT AWARENESS

Do you take notice of all that's happening around you, from significant to seemingly insignificant things? Or, do you let life pass in front of your eyes missing potential opportunities to capitalize on your growth?

Discovering and re-inventing yourself is a whole lot easier when you practice awareness and self-awareness. Both of these traits are innate within all of us. However, sometimes there's a little work that needs to be done to reconnect with our awareness. It's common to feel distant with our awareness during some parts of our life. But the good thing? It doesn't have to be permanent. You have the power and courage to reconnect with just about anything that's within you innately. All you need to do is decide.

Awareness is the ability to recognize what's happening in the atmosphere around you. It gives you the opportunity to understand your character, feelings, and what inspires you. Your awareness will help you begin to realize the things that move you physically, emotionally, and mentally. It will most importantly allow you to see what you want to chase and follow. If we want to create change, if we want to design the trajectory of our life, we need to embrace our awareness. That starts now.

The goal of this section is to teach you different lessons I learned along my journey that reconnected me with my own awareness, and that can also reconnect you with yours. These chapters are a bundle of tools you can use to your advantage. Read each one carefully, then read the ones that resonate most more times if you'd like. You can always come back to these lessons, they're here for you and are yours forever. If something doesn't resonate, remember, that's completely okay.

These are instances and experiences that have helped my journey of self-discovery. But what worked for me, may not work the same for you. Take the things that feel right and incorporate those into your life. Whether you learn one or 100 lessons from this section, it's enough to create a positive shift in your life.

In this section, we will talk about a range of life aspects that relate to your awareness and self-awareness. Whether your journey is just beginning, or you have already found your purpose, these chapters can help you elevate your life in many ways. They're potentially the secret to using awareness to help unlock your greatest potential and become the best version of yourself. To get you started on the right foot, here's an overview of the lessons and topics we will discuss:

- **How journaling can become your best tool**
- **The importance of noticing the small things**

- **What honest self-questioning can do for you**
- **How to adapt to your surroundings**
- **The power of stillness and silence**

Although these lessons are a collection of my life experiences, there was a time in my life when I was far from self-aware. It was common for me to carelessly go through life, missing opportunities to change the way I was living for the better. I never spent time focusing on cultivating my awareness, partially because I didn't understand its importance. It wasn't until my solo backpacking trip in Europe that I started to come in touch with my innate awareness. I slowly learned that the more aware I could be, the more control I could have over the direction of my life. Once I had that understanding, I committed to holding my level of awareness as one of my highest priorities.

Maybe you've never even heard of awareness or considered it a crucial part of your journey, and that's okay. It's never too late to connect with your awareness. It's always the right time.

#2
YOUR FIRST STEP IS MOST CRUCIAL

The first thing I always tell people to do when they're beginning the journey of self-discovery is to buy a journal. We all want to uncover our innate riches. We want to come across the gold mine that will give us our dream life. We crave understanding what will take us to the next level.

You're probably asking, "Why a journal?" Yeah, I get it. A couple hundred pieces of blank paper definitely doesn't have any predetermined answers written out to help you find what you need. But that's exactly why I always recommend to start with a journal. The pages are blank, waiting for you to begin writing your story. No other author, professor, or coach has put their words down to guide you. A journal gives you access to the author's chair. It puts opportunity in your hands. It gives your brain the chance to set its own path.

The purpose behind the journal is for you to put everything down. From the daily bullshit you're going through, to your triumphs, to the shitty coffee you had yesterday and how you'll never return to the same coffee shop, to your hot date last night, and, even sometimes, to why you don't give a shit about writing anything down on a particular day. You'll slowly see how it's going to teach you a lot about yourself.

You're going to dig into what you love, what you hate, people you aspire to be like, people you want to surround yourself with, and people you never want to see again. It's going to give you the opportunity to write stories about your childhood, about the crazy college days, and possibly even your future—things you never would have written about if you hadn't taken the initial step of buying a journal.

I tell people that writing will open them up to an entire world they never knew existed. Kind of like Narnia. Minus the bookcase and cold weather…yet similar in unexpectedness and amazement. If you just sit down and *try*, you'll be blown away. Things will come out of your pen that you wouldn't have thought of by just sitting down and trying to think of ideas.

A journal gives you the opportunity to write, but it's a bit more in-depth than that. It can serve as the first opportunity you have to dabble with self-awareness. It can be a teacher of, well, yourself. It can bring things forward you didn't know ever existed. But, again, it doesn't just happen. There's no shortcut. It takes practice and consistency. It takes repetition, day after day. Over time, you'll find a rhythm. You'll find a beat. You'll begin to groove.

Let me help you a bit because it's challenging from the beginning, especially if this is completely new to your life. I had guidance from the beginning. But since then, I've found what works and doesn't work for me. I've nailed down the most efficient things to write about to help you become aware.

I get it. It's hard to figure out where to start. What do you write about? How long do you write for? These are the questions I get all the time when people decide to buy their first journal.

When people ask me for guidance or help with their journaling, I give them the prompts that allowed me to unlock my self-awareness. These prompts are writing practices that help me understand my character, my feelings, and what leads me to the gateway of self-awareness.

We're all self-aware, but we need to be reminded that we are. That's what these exercises did for me. They allowed me to brainstorm my own life—past, present, and future—and figure out the opportunities waiting for me. Without these prompts, I would be lost.

I want these prompts to serve you the same as they did me. I want them to be your hope, your first glimpse of becoming you. I want them to not only teach you in the beginning, but also become exercises you can return to when you're further along your path.

These prompts are meant to be the initial gold mines. Take your pick axe and begin to uncover your riches. Understand yourself, your feelings, what moves you both physically and emotionally, and what life opportunities exist if you look within.

VERBAL VOMIT

The first prompt is something I like to call verbal vomit. Yes, vomit. The goal is to "vomit" any words from your mind onto your journal. It's an exercise that allows the brain to get moving. It allows the gears to start turning.

There are two rules to this exercise. Rule #1 is to write without thinking and get anything down on paper. Rule #2 is just as important. If you break rule #2, Lord have mercy. Rule #2 is to not break rule #1.

Seriously, don't do it.

The goal of this exercise is to get you writing. As you work through this exercise, things will come to you that are new. Maybe you'll randomly start to write about how you love practicing self-growth, or maybe you'll write about why you get stressed, or maybe you'll even write an entire story of your childhood. The amazing thing about this exercise is it serves as the ultimate release and can lead you to new discoveries of yourself.

There was a time when one of my closest friends got what I like to call a "dream job." In my mind, he had it made. He was doing exactly what he wanted and, more importantly, he loved doing it. But I was completely turned off by his achievement and didn't want anything to do with it or him because I was sinking in a pool of jealousy. It seemed I'd never reach a point where I could be proud of him.

After swimming in that self-doubt, I turned to this exercise. I began by writing what I was feeling and why I was experiencing those feelings. I was writing things that never previously came to mind. In the beginning, I was writing a lot of negative emotions about this situation. But about half way through, something clicked.

I began to write about how everyone has the ability to choose which lens we see life through. It's up to us. And in that situation, I was looking at life through a lens of jealousy. I was filtering out all the positive opportunities to feel motivated and all I could see or feel was jealously.

So, I made the decision to look at it through a lens of inspiration. I began to realize if he could do what he loves for a living, then so could I. His achievement validated that we all have the same opportunity to do what we love, we just need to create a space for the opportunity to arise.

By taking a step back and utilizing a verbal vomit exercise, I was able to change my lens of jealousy to a lens of inspiration. It gave me a new perception that helped me find out how to create space for a similar opportunity. It led me to become more aware about what I was experiencing, and gave me a better understanding of my feelings and what moves me physically, emotionally, and mentally.

GRATITUDE JOURNALING

Gratitude: the quality of being thankful; the ability to show appreciation and to return kindness. Having a mindset that revolves around gratitude takes practice. Through this practice you become immensely aware, you learn what gives you joy. And, more importantly, it can help you view life through a brand new lens that allows you to find appreciation in almost everything.

Gratitude is innate within all of us, we just need to find ways to tap into it. It's not a foreign way of living, it's actually quite practical. And, if you can find out what you're most grateful for, you'll know what you need to keep in your life. If those things aren't uncovered, it can be tough to nail down what direction we want to go on our path of self-discovery.

Gratitude can serve as a guide, a flashlight that shines down your path when the light at the end of the tunnel is non-existent. Gratitude can be a teacher, it can be *your* teacher. It can be my teacher. And, it can be our teacher.

Gratitude is something that will always be here, even as trends come and go. It allows all of us to encounter some of our deepest desires. Gratitude opens up a field of happiness and helps us appreciate our surroundings. From the leaves on the ground beneath a tree to the water that trickles down a creek to the summer breeze that cools the air, gratitude gives us the opportunity to realize all the things we could (and should) be thankful for.

As you slowly tap into your reservoir of gratitude, your awareness is going to flourish. You'll have realizations of the things that bring you the most joy. You'll have encounters with aspects of your life you never thought you could be thankful for. Like your cup of coffee, or the pen that lets you write in your journal, or the ability to cook food. These are all things we can be grateful for, but a lot of us don't spend enough time focusing on them because they seem insignificant.

To begin my journey of finding gratitude in my own life, I began to use gratitude journaling, an exercise taught to me by my brother, Evan. Before it, I had no clue what it meant to be grateful. But I embraced this new practice, and I challenge you to do the same.

Gratitude journaling only has to take two or three minutes every day. There's really no excuse to *not* do it. Plus, there are really only five steps to gratitude journaling. Okay maybe six, but each of them could take you less than 30 seconds to do.

Confused? Overwhelmed? Seem a bit too hard? I hope not, but if that's the case, don't panic. Everything is fine. I get it. It seems like a ton of steps and you're probably uncertain how this would take less than three minutes to do every morning. But, I promise you, it's much easier than it sounds and you'll pick it up after the first go around. Let me simplify things for you.

Gratitude journaling consists of writing five things:

1. Something you're grateful for that happened yesterday
2. Something you're grateful for today
3. One thing you're looking forward to today
4. Someone you're grateful for from your childhood
5. One seemingly insignificant item you're grateful for that's in front of you

Once you write those five things, you're just about done. The first five steps are wonderful, and you could probably be pretty content with just those. But there's something about the human mind that likes hearing positive affirmations every day. The more we tell ourselves positive things, even if they have yet to happen, the more likely we are to live a life that encompasses them.

The final step of this journal exercise is to write the same positive affirmation every day after you create your gratitude list. There's no right or wrong affirmation to jot down. It could be as simple as "I'm happy and successful," or it could trend toward a larger manifestation like "I wake up to live a creative life and empower others to use their voice to its full potential." Really, this one is up to you.

Think of it this way: Positive affirmations are an opportunity for you to seize any negative thoughts and manifest a new reality into existence. They may be considered something along the line of unrealistic or wishful thinking, but they're powerful. When you repeat positive affirmations often, and believe in them, you can start to shape your life in a way that creates positive changes to make those statements your reality.

GUIDED BRAINSTORM

In a nutshell, a guided brainstorm is an exercise that builds a pathway to reaching an ultimate answer you've been seeking. The beauty of this journal exercise is that you can use it to help you find answers to a wide variety of questions.

Personally, I used a guided brainstorm to help find my purpose—the reason I'm on this planet. But besides that, you could use it to help you discover the type of partner you need in your life, your passions, or your favorite food. Literally anything. It can help you navigate down a path of uncertainty to a field of opportunity.

It's pretty simple, too. Take a question, any question you want to work on answering, then use a bullet list to help brainstorm anything and everything in your life that potentially relates to your question. Because it plays a large role in this masterclass, and it's a hot question many people tend to ask, we will go ahead and use this as our example: "What's my purpose?"

This is how I began to discover what my purpose in life was—the real reason and motivator to get out of bed every day, fueled with energy. I asked myself this question and wrote down everything that came to mind that related to why I believe I'm here. The goal: compile the bullet list into one succinct sentence that provides an answer to the question. So, for me, my goal was to become aware of my purpose. But more importantly, to find one sentence that embodied everything I stand for and value.

Here is a look at my exact guided brainstorm session:

What's your purpose? What's your reason for getting out of bed every morning?

- *Writing*
- *Creating*
- *Inspiring people*
- *Showing people they're not alone*
- *Empowering people to use their voice*
- *Creating space for others*
- *Prioritizing community*
- *Showing people it's okay to have feelings*

- *Motivating people to create space for opportunity*
- *Showing people they can do whatever they want*
- *Storytelling*
- *Inspiring people to adventure*
- *Inspiring people to learn more about themselves*
- *Inspiring people to be their true selves*
- *Being vulnerable to encourage others to open up*

What a list. Long and filled with great ideas, but that list doesn't really cut it. I'm not going to pull out my laundry list every time I want to remind myself why I'm here. From the bullet points, you'll need to find the overarching theme. How can you summarize all those points into one succinct and powerful sentence? That's exactly what you need to ask yourself.

But don't panic, sometimes you need to let this exercise simmer for a bit. It's okay to sit on that list and just ponder. Read through your list until it comes to you or maybe new ideas will pop into your head as time progresses. Whatever your process involves, just learn to enjoy it. Learn to appreciate the struggle you have to go through to find your answer. Because in life, it's the things we enjoy struggling for that provide us the most happiness.

I sat with my list for a week and read it every morning to hopefully get those gears cranking again. It took me a while. I'm not going to lie, my answer didn't come easy. I struggled and struggled, but I learned to love that process. I knew what was to come, so it made the preceding steps feel valuable. To help, I tried to find three common themes on my list.

I found there were a lot of references to creating, adventuring, and people on my list. I believed those could be the foundation of my succinct, one sentence answer. I slowly began to piece the puzzle together. I wrote down what I thought my purpose was and then immediately scratched it. It just didn't fit, and that's okay.

You may run into the same challenge. But keep your head down and sit with your list for a while. I let my list sink in for days. One morning something fell into place. It was one of those "when you know, you know" moments. It came forward in my mind, and I immediately knew that this guided brainstorm had led me to become aware of my purpose.

I discovered my answer: *I wake up each morning to live a creative and adventurous life and encourage others to be the best versions of themselves.*

So, take your time with this exercise. Great things don't happen overnight. But I assure you, this is a guide you can rely on to find answers to things in life that are most important to you.

> **JOURNALING CAN BE THE MAGNIFYING GLASS INTO YOUR OWN LIFE.**

#3
NOTICE EVERYTHING, EVEN THE SMALL THINGS

I once took a mindfulness class at a high-level university, and learned a few things. First off, I learned that I wouldn't necessarily recommend it to a friend because it taught me that we are all innately mindful. We don't need someone to teach us how to be mindful. Save yourself a few hundred bucks, please. However, there still were some valuable lessons in the few classes I attended, which I want to share with you.

Second off, I learned that when I eat anything, I'm never focused on the taste, the sensation, the temperature, or the texture. I tend to forget to breathe when I eat. Have you ever tried to chew a piece of food 21 times before swallowing it? I've heard it's a good way to slow down your eating, but I found it doesn't align with my "forget to breathe" eating approach.

One of the first exercises we did in that class involved bringing a grape to the lecture. Not something you'd usually think to bring to a college-level class. Well, at least for me it's not. My lecture essentials usually were a pen and paper to pretend to take notes with, a laptop to also pretend to take notes with (but really just use to surf the web), and imaginary ear plugs to get me through the hour lecture. As you can tell, lectures were on the bottom of my totem pole of important things.

This time around, we were going to do an eating exercise, a little different than the eating exercises I preferred in my college lectures. I would bring snacks to help pass the time. You know, like every 15 minutes I would dive back in for another handful of those salty almonds or try and quietly wrestle the foil wrapper off a sugar filled protein bar. But, for this class, we would be using our grapes for an exercise to help us become more aware.

To start the exercise, we closed our eyes and slowly put the grape in our mouth. Then, we gently bit into the grape allowing the grape juice to spurt out. As that happened, we were to focus with great attention on everything. From the flavor to the temperature of the juice to how it felt against the inside of our cheeks to the sound the grape's skin made as our teeth slowly punctured its edges. We became aware of everything and anything to do with the grape in that moment.

I tried to make sense of it all. I asked myself, "What's the overarching purpose of this exercise?" We weren't just learning about a grape and its potential for providing a sweet burst of juice. No, that's too shallow. There had to be more. If you're like me, I like to investigate things in life on a deeper level. In this case, I was on a mission in my mind to find out what the hell this grape embodied. What could it be related to in my life or, even better, *our* lives? Pretty much anything.

The burst of the grape's juice can be a parallel to almost everything in life. It can symbolize the moment you release all the stress you've been carrying around for years because you feel the need to take on everyone else's problems so people can see you as a "good person." It can represent that feeling of joy when you break through a wall of overwhelm built up from years of trying to please everyone around you before taking care of yourself. It can illustrate that rush of happiness you receive when you are doing exactly what you love with no worries of judgement from others or challenges from overthinking. It can teach you about your feelings, character, and what moves you physically, emotionally, and mentally. It can teach you awareness. But even better, it can teach you *self-awareness.*

As you move through your life and create your own story, remember to focus on what's going on at all times—the obvious things and even the not so obvious things, like the grape juice or what causes certain emotions to arise. Know that sometimes those seemingly insignificant things can teach you a great deal about yourself and others around you.

"

THE SMALL THINGS IN LIFE TEACH THE MOST PROFOUND LESSONS.

#4
HONEST SELF-QUESTIONING

How often do you run in circles around your daily problems because you can't find a solution to your struggles? Hmm, that one hit home I bet. What if I told you that the reason you can't find solutions is because you're too afraid to ask the right questions?

The right questions are ones that hurt to ask and also hurt to answer. They don't just scrape the surface, they go much deeper than that. They don't make you feel like you're running through a field of wildflowers singing Lucy in the Sky with Diamonds wondering if Paul McCartney was actually tripping on LSD. No, the right questions make you contemplate your actions retrospectively, presently, and on a go-forward basis. They make you understand why the hell you've been feeling like shit or why you get so frantic when someone disagrees with you or when someone doesn't show you love or when your family doesn't call you back or when you just have no idea who you are.

If I could choose the voice that's always in my head, I would make it the voice of *honest self-questioning*. This voice would ask the deeper questions when I'm too afraid to do so myself. We all want the easy way out, and having this voice play a role in our daily lives could help us take the road less traveled. It could push us in new directions by forcing us to not only understand our boundaries, but also break through them.

In a perfect world, the voice of honest self-questioning and I would have daily conversations that would most likely piss me off because I wouldn't want to answer the questions. However, it would be the same as when you don't want to do something your mother says, but then you realize that moms know everything. The voice of honest self-questioning is in that same realm. It just always seems to know what questions to ask.

For example, I was contemplating if I had the talent to learn an instrument and be a beginner even though thus far in my life it seemed I wasn't born with the talent of becoming a musician. It seemed like I was too far behind to start, and the market of musicians was too saturated.

The voice of honest self-questioning then asked me, "Does someone always know they were born with a specific talent?" I sat there in silence and realized that not only does the voice of honest self-questioning ask introspective questions, but it also makes me think of answers that move me and give me the extra kick I need.

In response to that question I replied (in my head), "Actually, no. You must do the work to figure out that you were born with a talent." This was the moment I realized everything is worth trying, and it was all because of honest self-questioning. It all came from asking a question I didn't want to face, but in the end it provided me the answer I needed to hear. It pushed me to test my ability to chase a new endeavor.

That's the beauty of life. It's a constant game of trying to find your calling. The only way to find your calling is to be extremely curious. Be curious about things you know how to do, but also be curious about things you have no idea how to do. You may not know something is innate until you give it a go.

I believe that's what honest self-questioning can do for all of us. Whatever you may be trying to figure out, whether it's understanding your own emotions, discovering a hidden talent, learning what triggers you and how to avoid those triggers, what things in life you should dedicate all of your energy to, what things in life you should not dedicate your energy to, or anything you want to find out about yourself that you can't figure out by floating through life like a dandelion hoping that one day the sun will just decide to shine brighter on you and feed you the answers to your happiness.

Whether you're an honest self-questioning ninja or a fish out of water, I think it's fair to agree example questions would be beneficial. Here are different situations that we often encounter, and the questions I use to help me improve my self-awareness and work through these challenges:

1. **Emotional triggers:**
   What triggers your emotions most? What are some positive actionable steps you can take to overcome those triggers moving forward?

2. **Happiness, gratitude, and enthusiasm:**
   What in life makes you vibrate with happiness and gratitude? What in life energizes you and fills you with enthusiasm?
3. **Overcoming pain and finding forgiveness:**
   When somebody hurts you, how do you not let the pain destroy the walls of your heart? How do you move toward forgiveness?
4. **Understanding incorrect societal assumptions:**
   What does society say you must do that you don't agree with? Have you thought that maybe society has the wrong answers and you can go against the grain?
5. **Accepting that failure can be a positive:**
   What's worse, trying and failing, or not trying and wondering what could have been?
6. **Starting today and not tomorrow:**
   How many times have you told yourself today is the day you would start?
7. **Avoiding saying something negative:**
   What if you took a deep breath before saying something negative? What if you took a minute to sit with your feelings before reacting?
8. **Believing anything is possible:**
   Why settle for less in a universe defined by infinity?
9. **Searching for opportunity:**
   Are you creating space for opportunity? What actions can you instill in your life that can help more opportunities arise?

10. Relying on intangibles:
Do you rely on honest relationships, your heart, intuition, patience, and positive affirmations? Or, do you only rely on tangible things?

Honest self-questioning is a way to examine your own actions and motives, which can create a new world of self-awareness. These types of questions can be the magnifying glass into the parts of your life you've yet to explore. They can zoom in on your insecurities.

Honest self-questioning will take your insecurities and teach you to embrace them with open arms and an open mind. You'll begin to see these areas are opportunities for growth and improvement instead of things you should run from. You'll learn to be proud of your insecurities because your imperfections create your natural beauty.

We must understand the answers we desire usually come from asking daunting questions. Let uncovering your own riches be your reward for overcoming your intimidation of these questions. You never know which question is going to give you the solution you've been seeking, so don't stop asking. Don't. Stop. Asking.

Before you go telling yourself you don't need to ask honest self-questions because your life seems all pretty and happy, let me request one thing: never say you've learned everything you need to know about yourself. I promise you there's always something more to learn and explore about your own being.

One of the most important things in life is dedicating yourself to yourself. Give yourself permission to explore your inner being before trying to figure out the external forces that surround you. By asking these raw and real questions, you can guide yourself down your own path, a path with no footprints and a lot of room to run wild.

With every question you ask, let your answer be your next foot forward. Let your answer be one piece of your puzzle. Let your answer motivate you to keep on running. You deserve this shit.

> **WHY SETTLE FOR LESS IN A UNIVERSE DEFINED BY INFINITY?**

#5
ADAPT TO YOUR SURROUNDINGS

It's common to miss out on golden opportunities because most of the time they require you to change something in your life. Not only that, but sometimes you aren't even aware of new opportunities or instances of change that would benefit you. Whether that's because you are completely oblivious or distracted by other nuisances, it really doesn't matter. Regardless, you miss those opportunities. But it doesn't have to be like that.

You can train yourself to recognize those opportunities and tap into them based on feelings and indicators—your awareness. However, you can also fall into the trap of resistance and be hesitant to capitalize on the opportunities of growth, prosperity, and becoming your true self. I'm assuming you'd prefer the former.

To be able to tap into those opportunities, you must learn how to avoid the trap of resistance. Resistance is a daily enemy you must figure out. It's a puzzle within the larger puzzle of life. Many times, you resist change because it makes you feel uncomfortable, uneasy, overwhelmed, stressed out, and a ton of other feelings. The thing is, at the very same time, changes that make you feel all those emotions may be the ones worth accepting.

First, before jumping on the train to change, you need to be able to recognize that there's this new path of opportunity. You need to get in tune with your own body and the feelings that arise when something new or different is tossed your way.

Instead of dodging change, you need to let it hit you and take you where you're supposed to go. Usually, though, you'll do all you can to resist being hit by those changes. Without even knowing it, you've trained your brain that comfortability is the absolute best state you can live in. But all that's really doing to you is building up a brick wall that represents your fear of adapting to a new path of life that may have opportunities you thought existed only in your dreams.

For me, the telltale sign that I should chase something is when something makes me question my identity, feel emotions I've never felt before, and think that I'm not supposed to do it because I've never tried it before. Really, when I encounter something that has the potential of making me fail, I usually feel the need to go after it. Here's the thing: If there's a potential to fail, there's also an equal opportunity to succeed.

I've learned how to recognize those situations and instead of resisting them, I adapt to them. I've found ways to roll with them because I believe we get thrown into challenging and uncomfortable situations as tests from the universe.

Are you going to set yourself free and achieve your life's greatest potential? Or, are you going to sit there and remain the same? Easier said than done, but I think we all can agree that it's best if we exert all our effort during our finite time here. Unless you want to stay stagnant, work that job you sorta-kinda-like but definitely loathe deep down inside your heart, and run away from the opportunity of becoming the best version of you.

We need to accept that it's okay to adapt to these tests. We need to become aware of those feelings and emotions triggering in real time. Because if we can't, then we are leaving a lot of potential new doors closed. But I know, and I hope you know, that you're capable of capitalizing on this. You have the strength to buckle down and let life push you in the direction you're meant to be going. You just have to let go of the voice of self-doubt in your head. You need to trust your intuition. You need to understand that doing the same thing over and over again expecting different results is insanity (shout out to Albert Einstein).

So, be open to change. Accept a new and different path that's bound to bring you to an enlightened destination; somewhere you've never been, but somewhere you've always belonged.

Stop letting yourself make up excuses that are limiting your potential. You're more than good enough to do anything you want. You are a miracle capable of many other miracles. However, it's not always easy to recognize when life is trying to push you in a new direction. I still struggle with recognizing those moments myself. It's usually difficult to realize when life is asking you to adapt to something new when you're stuck doing something that's extremely familiar.

When you do the same thing every day and there aren't any true issues, it's challenging to recognize areas you can improve, change, or capitalize on. It's difficult to see how to take something to the next level if it feels like it's working well. Why would you shift directions if it's working? Because there's always potential for more. Much more.

I totally get it. Changing directions may not be as easy as it sounds. What it really comes down to is understanding some of the different signs in life that can tell you to go in a new direction. These indicators can guide you down a new path and let you become aware that it's time to adapt to your surroundings. Here are some ways life does its best to tell you it's time to shift gears:

1. WHEN SOMETHING YOU LOVE STARTS TO FEEL LIKE A CHORE

One of my biggest rules in life is the things you feel deeply passionate about should never feel like a chore. Never. You should always be willing to put in the extra work if they truly hold a special place in your heart. But that doesn't mean they can't begin to feel like a chore over time.

When something starts to feel like the last thing you want to do, you need to reconsider what you're doing, why you're doing it, and how you can change it up. This should be an immediate red flag. This is life's way of saying, "Hey! Anyone in there?! You used to love this stuff and now you loathe it. I think it's time to let go and move on to the next open door on your path. Come on, I'll try and show you the way." There's no need to answer, but there's also no need to resist.

Trust what the universe wants you to do. You're worthy of its guidance.

2. WHEN YOUR PROGRESSION HAS BECOME STAGNANT AND LINEAR

I think we all can agree that in a perfect world our progress and success would be a constant upward trend that never falls or goes in a million circles. Again, in a perfect world. But we don't live in a perfect world (news flash!). So, there are many times when your progression will go south and you'll begin to question just about everything, even your existence.

But stop, take a deep breath, observe what's happening, and process what you're going through. If you feel like your progression is stagnant, linear, or even heading south, this is a clear sign you need to change something up. Again, life's way of shouting, "Yo! Let's kick into gear buddy. You're falling behind. Time to shake it up, get ambitious, and do something different." Don't take this with a grain of salt. This is what you need. This is a sign that it's time to adapt to where life wants to take you.

3. WHEN YOU'RE CONSTANTLY DREAMING ABOUT THE PAST

We're all guilty of obsessing over the past. Admit it. One major problem of our world is most people don't live in the present moment. A few things are extremely toxic about not living in the present moment. First, it's a clear sign that you're not content with your current situation. Second, it represents a lack of gratitude for what you currently have in life.

Fantasizing about what has already happened serves no good purpose. Yeah, if you have accomplishments, don't just let them disappear. Always keep those close. But that doesn't mean milk them so long that they're your only focus until the end of time. View them as validation that you're worthy of many more successes.

After all is said and done, if you're dreaming about the past, that's a clear sign you need to shake your life up and move on. Life is knocking at your door and asking you to make some changes and adapt to your new surroundings. Maybe then, just maybe, you'll be able to achieve something greater than your past. You're worthy of the present moment.

4. WHEN YOUR DAILY ROUTINE ISN'T OPENING ANY NEW DOORS

Daily routines are great, don't get me wrong. I live and die by my routine. Without it, I'd probably be a bit insane, overwhelmed, and constantly stressed. Routines can be our anchor and safe place, protecting us when we encounter life's challenges. They can be our best friends, but they can also be our worst enemies.

I believe that setting yourself up to win the day is crucial to making immense progress with your personal and professional growth. However, I also believe it's important to not get too comfortable in our routines. That's when routines become an enemy.

Yes, it's important to get in a rhythm that keeps you moving forward. However, if that rhythm doesn't do anything but keep you stagnant or run you in circles, it's best to find a new beat to jive to.

Your daily routine should do a couple things. It should keep you in check, helping you complete and do whatever it is you need to do to remain mentally strong. It should let you win the day without any doubts or complications. It should continue opening new doors and pushing you to go for more.

If your routine feels boring and dry, it's probably a good idea to reconsider what you're doing daily. Again, that's a clear indicator that life's asking you to adapt to something new and different with hopes to push you in the right direction. People willing to alter their lives and bring in new energy are the ones with skyrocketing success. You can experience that too, but you need to be willing to drop your old patterns and trust the new.

5. WHEN YOU'RE SIMPLY UNHAPPY

It's impossible to be happy every minute of every day. Sure, we can pretend to be like that, but that's just us believing our own lies. That's the problem with this epidemic of positive attitudes nowadays. Half of the time people are just pretending their life is fine and dandy. However, that isn't reality. The truth is life's a professional shit disturber, and it's known to make us uncomfortable. If you're feeling unhappy, it's okay, but recognize it. Don't stuff it down and avoid it. Face it.

This is an obvious sign that there are aspects of your life you need to think about changing. Before you drown from the influx of guilt you feel from creating a lie, perceive this as an opportunity to adapt and change. Make a decision. Decide that you're ready to make a change in your life to bring real, natural happiness. Because choosing the convenient alternative of believing your own lies isn't a healthy decision.

Let's put it this way: You are not meant to stay the same for your entire life. You are meant to evolve. You are meant to level up. You are meant to continuously grow into the best version of yourself. You are meant to discover new opportunities, chase them, and let them bring you to your next stepping stone.

Shift your mindset around change and see it as one of life's greatest gifts. Change is a chance for you to start fresh, tap into something new, and uncover more about your life. Don't back down when change introduces itself into your life. Smile that it arrived and let your willingness to adapt to your surroundings take you to places you belong.

> **TRUST WHAT THE UNIVERSE WANTS YOU TO DO. YOU'RE WORTHY OF ITS GUIDANCE.**

#6
WHEN IN DOUBT, CLOSE YOUR EYES

For most of my life I was "too cool for school." Fitting in was a big worry of mine; I was always in a popularity contest in my head. Not only that, but I don't think I ever felt like I was winning the contest. Now that I look back at those times with wiser eyes, maybe that was a good thing. There were, and still are, repercussions from trying to live out that kind of life. It made me considerably entitled internally.

There are a few issues to entitlement: 1) you believe you're always right, 2) your ego prevents you from admitting you're wrong, 3) you resist asking yourself the honest questions because truthfulness scares you shitless, and 4) you lack awareness and self-awareness. Oh yeah, one more thing: you don't give others the opportunity to share advice or offer up other helpful solutions.

That was me in a nutshell. Internally, at least. I'm not sure if I truly exposed it. It wasn't until a year or two ago that I realized listening to what other people have to say is only going to open your mind to new things, different routes of life, and tools to discover yourself and your journey.

YOUDESERVETHISSHIT

When I first heard of meditating, I was in the "I want to do what everyone else does" phase of my life. Sounded like some pretty woo-woo spiritual shit. Not necessarily my cup of tea at the time. But, luckily, I changed. Things began to shift for me as I progressed along my own journey, and they can also shift for you. I came to a point in my life where I wanted to do unique things. I wanted to be a unique individual. I, for the first time in my life, wanted to be different. Yes, *different*.

So, what did I do? I started to listen to other people as a source of medicine. Specifically, though, my partner encouraged me to give meditation a shot. At first, my old patterns were triggered and I wasn't ready to listen. But then I decided to drop my ego and just listen. Yes, *listen*.

I began to open up to the idea of meditation because I was having trouble finding the answers I wanted. I guess you can say it was my last hope to become fully aware. Well, that's a bit extreme. We're all self-aware and mindful, but sometimes we just need something to bring it back to the surface. Those things often get pushed to the wayside, which is okay as long as you find the motivation to reconnect with them.

For me, meditation became a highway to reconnecting with my self-awareness. I was in dire need of rejuvenating my mind, body, and spirit. It was time to go back to the basics and look within. It was time to use my own energy to help solve my own complications. This practice completely changed my life, and it's still changing my life every time I choose to shut my eyes and quiet my mind. The lessons I learn in silence are unmatched. It's simply a miracle.

I understand that meditation may seem pretty woo-woo. Sounds a bit weird to be honest, but I encourage you to just give it a shot if you haven't yet. I challenge you to try it at least three times a week for one month. Sounds intimidating, I know, but it's a healthy challenge.

I'm confident that you can find something that works because there's a method for everyone. We just need to excavate what's already there, kind of like magic. It may not come quick for some, but remember: Great things don't happen overnight. Your greatest discovery is just around the corner. I can't guarantee how many corners you'll have to go around before then, but I encourage you to never stop.

So, great, I'm asking, challenging, encouraging, and motivating you to look within and meditate. But you're probably thinking, *how?* Valid question, thank you for asking so kindly. Here are some meditation practices I've experimented with and found beneficial:

1. GRATITUDE MEDITATION – FOCUS ON WHAT YOU'RE THANKFUL FOR

Here we are again talking about gratitude. First, we learned about practicing what we are grateful for through journaling, which is a very active practice involving movement and thought. Now, we are digging a bit deeper into the topic through a way that could probably be considered the exact opposite of journaling.

Gratitude meditation is a practice encompassing complete silence. There's no movement, and you avoid any unwanted thoughts besides those that accompany our desire to feel grateful. There are tons of guided meditations nowadays that you can access in less time than it takes to open a social media app to distract yourself from doing something worth your time. So, take 10 minutes and make them yours.

Gratitude meditation, similar to gratitude journaling, can help you find answers to the things you need to know but won't know until you meditate on the things you are most thankful for. You'll realize what in your life you've taken for granted, which are most often things you'll feel encouraged to take more time appreciating.

Gratitude meditation is all about focusing on the good while shielding out life's challenges for a few moments of time. It's not often we can shut off the outside world and focus on what it is we really are thankful for in life. However, you can make this happen more often by looking within and feeling your emotions around the things in life you can't live without.

2. MANIFESTATION MEDITATION – BRING YOUR DREAMS INTO EXISTENCE

I heard a story about a young adult who had pinpointed exactly what he wanted in his life, but he wasn't sure of the proper steps he would need to take to get there. It was as if he had the puzzle, knew the end result, but was unable to come remotely close to putting the pieces in their right places. He couldn't find where they belonged, so he was about ready to give up and accept the kind-of-okay-but-not-that-great life he was living.

He had heard stories about some of the most successful people in the world manifesting their dreams into existence. Literally dreams and visions within their heads became their everyday realities. This seemed somewhat magical, but he couldn't resist trying it on himself and seeing what would happen.

Every morning for a month this young man shut his eyes and listened to the same guided manifestation meditation. He treated it like a class, and you should too. Sitting there listening to his teacher (the guided meditation), he chose one thing he wanted to manifest into his life. In other words, he chose one thing that was a dream that he wanted to make a reality.

With his eyes shut and his mind somewhat turned off, he decided he wanted to bring his dream of being a writer into existence. He wanted that to be real. He thought of every detail of the visions he had with writing. He made sure he was aware of every little thing about that dream.

Over the course of these "classes" or morning manifestations, he became completely aware of the specific steps he needed to take in life to get him there. At first, he was skeptical of this woo-woo bullshit, but then it slowly became something he couldn't live without. He couldn't find a good enough excuse not to attend his class and meet with his teacher every morning. And his homework? Well, it had no due dates, but it was up to him to go and act on those things he uncovered in his meditations. So he did.

Every new thing he found out while looking within, he made sure he responded with an action in life. Slowly over time, he began to see his dream becoming more attainable. It was becoming more and more real one day at a time. It was *manifesting*. Although he was getting worn out from listening to the same meditation every day, there was too much proof of it working for him to stop.

For him, this was a life changing moment. Who knows where he would be if he hadn't taken the steps to try this guided manifestation. The kid did great and eventually achieved exactly what he was visualizing in those meditations. Not only did he bring his dream of being a writer into existence, but he excavated the magic behind the ability we all have to live the exact life we want. He learned that you must sacrifice your time to get there; you can't just wait around for things to happen thinking you deserve this shit.

This is my story.

3. SILENT MEDITATION – QUIET THE NOISE WITHIN YOUR MIND

If you're looking to really, *really* challenge yourself and become incredibly aware, then sit in silence. The thing is, complete silence is impossible. Sure you could turn off your TV, shut your doors, and send a message to your neighbors to tone it down, but you still won't be in complete silence. Don't forget about that voice in your head telling you that you're not good enough. Don't forget about those thoughts reminding you about the little mistake you made the other day. Don't forget about the constant self-talk we do without even realizing.

So, even if everything is "silent" around you, your mind remains loud. It's a different kind of loud, though. It's a noise only we can hear. We must train ourselves how to shut it off.

We have no on and off switch in the beginning, but there can be eventually. That's why it's called a practice. You must put in the work and time to achieve something great.

Through silent meditation, which is literally sitting in silence with your eyes closed (could you have guessed?), we can train our minds to progressively become quieter and quieter and quieter. We have the power and ability to create a mental on and off switch.

But what's the power in becoming silent? Silence allows you shut off the outside world, creating space to become aware of the things that matter: feelings, emotions, your body, your mind, and even realizations about your life that can guide you down a new pathway.

Silent meditation is by no means easy. It's meant for those who want to achieve a unique kind of awareness. However, there are a few things to know that can help you on this silent journey: 1) use your breath as a focus point to drown out the outside world and connect to yourself, 2) one minute is just as good as 10 minutes, you'll be able to go longer as you practice, 3) trust yourself, and 4) embrace, appreciate, and enjoy the rare silence.

Are you ready to elevate your awareness?

Those meditation practices are just the beginning. Although the path of meditation can be long, it sure as hell is beneficial. Meditation is one way we can prepare ourselves for our future. It allows us to strip back our egos and cultivate a profound state of nothingness. In these times of quiet minds, we're able to achieve a glimpse into enlightenment. From that enlightened state, we can slowly become more aware of our surroundings and our body.

Meditation takes effort. This will be no walk in the park, just like the rest of this book. You can't just shut your eyes one morning and immediately become the Buddha. You must work through the difficulties of the practice to achieve greatness. Treat it like a class and show up every day with the intent to learn, with the intent to strive to become the best version of yourself.

This is a choice. This is *your* choice. If you want to make changes in your life and become aware of what steps you need to take, then decide. Decide that you deserve this shit—the exact life you want. Sacrifice your time so you become deserving. Sacrifice your time for meditation.

This is the beauty of meditation: We often find what we are looking for when we close our eyes and open our minds. So, when you're having doubts about becoming aware, close your eyes.

> YOU WERE CREATED TO DO GREAT THINGS, NOW'S YOUR TIME TO SHINE.

#7 AWARENESS: WHAT YOU CAN DO WITH THESE LESSONS

I'd be crazy to think you could remember everything in the last section and be able to implement it into your life immediately. Introducing new habits, practices, and ways of living into your life is challenging. I've done a lot of it and continue to do so. For me, having actionable steps or items I can follow helps me to implement changes successfully. If I'm not mistaken, you're probably in the same boat. I want to guide you in a direction that can help you feel motivated and enthusiastic about pursuing awareness.

In this chapter, I will lay out different action steps that relate to the previous chapters you've read. These actions are things you can do *today*. They don't require much work, besides your willingness to offer your conscious efforts. Don't be afraid to revisit a chapter, you can never learn too much about these actions that can make you become more aware:

1. **Buy a journal and begin a daily journaling practice:** Journaling is an excellent way to learn more about yourself and focus on a lot of aspects we tend to overlook, including what you're grateful for. To start, use one of the three journaling exercises I explained: verbal vomit, gratitude journaling, or a guided brainstorm. (Chapter 2)

2. **Notice the small things in life:** It's easy for us to go through life only focusing on the important things. However, don't forget about the seemingly insignificant things like the texture of your food, the joy you feel when you accomplish a goal, the stress you never want to admit you carry, or how you feel when someone uses a specific tone of voice. As you begin to take note of all the small things in life, you'll begin to open a new door to your awareness and find ways to improve certain areas of your life. (Chapter 3)

3. **Begin asking yourself honest questions:** Don't get me wrong, I never said asking yourself honest questions was easy, but I did say it's crucial. Although these questions are typically hard to ask yourself, they will give you opportunities to uncover life-changing answers. Begin to ask yourself questions about your life, happiness, stress, grief, and actions. This can be a way to learn more about yourself, as it allows you to examine your own actions and motives in life. (Chapter 4)

4. **Adapt and evolve to your surroundings:** As your awareness increases, you'll start to realize that life

may be urging you to move in a specific direction. Take notice of this and evolve with that urge. Don't resist going where life is asking you to go. Most of the time we hit a growth ceiling because we are too wary of where life wants to take us and choose to remain the same. However, when we let go and adapt to our surroundings we can go to unimaginable places. (Chapter 5)

5. **Create a meditation practice:** Meditation can be difficult, but that doesn't mean it's impossible. The value you can find within stillness is indescribable. If you're looking to challenge yourself and implement a new practice into your routine, choose meditation. There are several different types of meditation—silent, manifestation, gratitude—that can help you discover answers to your own life by looking within. Start small and work your way up to a consistent, everyday practice. If you need help, ask. (Chapter 6)

Remember, don't discount yourself. You are more than capable of acting on these five items. Although they may feel challenging at first, your small repeated actions will slowly move mountains in your life. If you want to create change, you need to take charge. You need to become responsible for your actions and begin to act on things that will create positive change. These five items can serve as your first efforts to create that positive change. I believe in you. But that doesn't matter. You know what matters? If you believe in yourself.

99

WHO DO YOU WANT TO BECOME?

PART II
COMFORT ZONES

To create space for opportunity, we must exit our safe zones and challenge ourselves to stand for uniqueness. Everything in life begins to flourish outside our comfort zones. That's where the magic happens.

#8
WHAT YOU'LL LEARN ABOUT COMFORT ZONES

Are you comfortable with being uncomfortable? Most likely not. From a young age, we crave and appreciate comfort. I'm also not wrong in saying that many people who envision living a comfortable life will do almost anything in their power to avoid being uncomfortable.

But whether you believe it or not, achieving any goal—especially the goal of discovering yourself—will require you to put yourself in some sort of uncomfortable situation or position. It's a truth not many people initially want to believe because it's typically a test of our boldness and ability to embrace new challenges.

Your comfort zone is the place you feel *most* comfortable. It's a stress-free zone where you know there will be no unexpected surprises or events. Although it's in our nature to retreat to this zone, it shouldn't be in our best interest.

Exponential personal and professional growth typically happens by putting ourselves in unique situations that will challenge us to become better. These situations likely *never* exist in our comfort zone. It may be difficult to understand at first, but it's crucial to chase something unfamiliar that keeps you on your toes.

Constant newness in your life will allow you to adapt to your surroundings and learn how to overcome difficult situations, ones that push you further along in your journey.

The goal of this section is to show you the power of living outside your comfort zone, how you can become comfortable with being uncomfortable, and actions that can help you get outside your comfort zone. It will teach you many lessons, but the overarching theme of each lesson is *standing for uniqueness*.

When you stand for uniqueness, you choose the life you want to live and not the life others make you believe you should live, or need to live. It's a frightening road to go down at first. However, after your first glimpse, you'll embrace the opportunities it brings to your life.

In this section, we'll discuss a plethora of lessons that you can use to live outside your comfort zone or, if you already do that, find more ways to challenge yourself to get further outside your comfort zone. Whether you've cracked the code to your life or you're just getting your feet wet, these chapters can serve as the guide to life outside your comfort zone.

The lessons within these chapters continue to change my life every day and encourage me to push further away from where I feel most comfortable. They're a foundation that reminds me that life is better lived in places that push your capabilities and show you your true worth. To get you well on your way to living a life outside your comfort zone, these are the seven lessons that will help you get started:

- Building trust with yourself
- How rejecting the normal can benefit you
- Feeling okay with being a beginner
- The power of curiosity
- Why complacency should be a red flag
- How you can benefit from failure
- Remove yourself from your familiar surroundings

Don't get me wrong, there was a large portion of my life where there was no chance I would do anything that put me outside my comfort zone. I think it's safe to say that's true for many people reading this book, possibly you. It's not innately within our nature to want to strive to do anything like that.

But I soon realized if I wanted to become who I was always meant to be, I needed to challenge myself to represent uniqueness. I didn't feel completely comfortable in my skin, and I began to realize the only way to change that was by putting myself outside my comfort zone. It was a difficult decision, but I found the energy to begin to live by those bold standards. Going outside my comfort zone changed my life.

Now, before I'm accused of something I didn't say, let's set something straight: Living outside your comfort zone may not fix or change your life immediately. However, the small, repeated actions you decide to take every day will soon result in something great, such as unlocking your greatest potential.

So, keep that in mind when you begin to implement these lessons into your own life.

It's the small but consistent work you add into your everyday life that will make groundbreaking changes over time. Be ready to take on unfamiliarity, it's going to become your new muse.

#9
BUILD TRUST WITH YOURSELF

Our natural instincts make it difficult for us to make rash decisions that will put us in uncomfortable situations. We are designed to retreat to safety when we feel danger, whether that danger threatens us physically or emotionally. We are creatures of comfort, which can prevent us from becoming the best versions of ourselves.

To have the courage to live outside our comfort zones, we must build trust with ourselves and continuously keep an eye on that trust level. Your ability to trust your own decisions determines how well and quickly you'll be able to navigate down your path.

How do you work on building trust and understanding your trust levels? Well, allow me to introduce you to your trust battery.

Your trust battery is a tool you can use to monitor the current level of trust between multiple people, or, more importantly, the level of trust you have with yourself. For the sake of this chapter and the lesson here, let's focus on using the trust battery with yourself rather than your surrounding community.

Your trust battery can indicate if you're lacking trust, or if your trust levels are through the ceiling. It will be the tool you can lean on when you're mustering up the trust to live a life outside your comfort zone.

Your trust battery works like this: every time life presents you with a challenge to do something outside your comfort zone, your battery is either charged or discharged. This means if you decide against doing something outside your comfort zone, your battery begins to deplete—you start to trust yourself less. However, if you do the opposite and choose to have the courage to live outside your comfort zone, your battery begins to charge—you begin to trust yourself more.

When your trust battery is high, it's easier to choose something outside your comfort zone. You have more confidence to live outside your comfort zone. When your trust battery is low, most challenging decisions and situations feel like pulling teeth. You're less likely to choose a life outside your comfort zone.

Without focusing on your trust battery, you run the risk of never building the necessary foundation to live a life outside your comfort zone. You won't understand the trust levels you have with yourself, and you'll most likely miss opportunities to push yourself to the limit and make progress on your path. It should be your new best friend. It's there for you and will guide you toward building the trust with yourself you've always wanted, as long as you do the work to constantly charge it.

When you start this type of work, your trust battery is around 50%. You have some trust with yourself, but you're not entirely there for yourself. You have moments of self-doubt. Over time, as life throws unfamiliar challenges at you, and if your decisions are positive, you begin to juice your battery up. However, with each negative decision—one where you let your self-doubt overtake you—your battery begins to drain.

The ultimate goal is to always charge your trust battery, even if it's full. There are different tips and tactics you can use to make sure it's continuously charging, whether it's already full or only at 50%. These practices can get you on the right track and help you charge your trust battery:

1. UNDERSTAND AND WORK WITH YOUR INNER CRITIC

The negative voice in your head can easily diminish your self-trust. While it's easy to believe what that voice says, it's crucial to not buy into it. That voice is known for creating issues of self-doubt, lack of motivation, and for depleting your trust battery. It may be difficult or even impossible to rule it out completely, but that doesn't mean we cannot work toward understanding its negativity.

Listen to your inner critic, but don't react to anything it tells you. See it as your own Devil's advocate, a voice that's doing all it can to pull you in the wrong direction. It will tell you that you're not worthy of something, and it will tell you to remain in your comfort zone, but don't let this voice push you away from building the trust you need to explore a life outside your comfort zone. We can never live without our inner critic, but we can learn to understand and work around it to reduce the impact it has on our self-trust.

2. CHALLENGE YOURSELF TO TRY SOMETHING NEW

Trying a new activity or hobby outside your comfort zone will help you charge your trust battery. Find something that challenges you in ways that are not familiar. The more often your try something new, the more self-trust you build to chase something outside your comfort zone.

When you try something new, start small. Give yourself time to adjust to this new way of living. It may feel challenging at first, but with time, you'll slowly fall in love with taking on new challenges, activities, or hobbies. These small acts will charge your trust battery and build your self-trust. You'll build the courage you need to attack life outside your comfort zone.

3. BE KIND TO YOURSELF

Your trust battery's best friend can be the words you feed your mind. Focusing on positive self-talk and embracing self-care is a quick way to cultivate self-trust. Positive self-talk and self-care are nutrients for your mind, body, and soul. Knowing that, you should always strive to be kind to yourself to help build the audacity to live outside your comfort zone.

The more pressure you put on yourself for not being good enough or not being confident, the quicker your trust battery will deplete. And that should never be the goal. Focus on positive affirmations—telling yourself positive statements—to help guide you toward a trust battery that's constantly full and charging. Through this practice, you will slowly see the power of self-kindness and reap the benefits of treating yourself as you wish to be treated by others.

Once you charge your trust battery and build enough trust in yourself to leave your comfort zone, you'll arrive at a completely new world. Your perception will shift, and you'll no longer feel the need to return to your comfort zone. The opportunities you'll get when you take that courageous step will change the way you approach life's challenges. You won't back down, you will rise up.

Trusting yourself is the first step in recognizing your full potential. Without that trust, living outside your comfort zone would be far from successful. There would be too many cases of self-doubt and subsequently retreating back to safety. It would be common for you to try something new and be only partially committed, which never yields success. If you really want it, you need to go for it. Give it your all. Forget about failure, forget about doubt, and forget about your sorry excuses that prevent you from becoming the best version of you.

Surprise yourself with your talents. Prove a new kind of worth to yourself and the world around you. Show your true colors and let it all go. Don't worry about the safety net of your comfort zone, you don't need that anymore. You'll have so many triumphs that a safety net will be the least of your worries. Your new worries will be finding the next challenging thing you'll achieve outside your comfort zone.

At its core, trust allows us to have faith in something. Trust builds an intention to believe that something is possible. The power of trust is always manifesting in our lives.

Your capabilities have always existed, but you can't uncover them until you trust and believe in yourself.

Trusting yourself is only the first step in seeing what's outside your comfort zone. It's the first thing we must do before rejecting the normal, striving for uniqueness, and going after exactly what we want to chase.

While many people will agree that it's the most difficult part of this journey, once you obtain that power of trust, you'll feel untouchable. You'll begin to wonder why you thought safety seemed like a better decision when your journey of self-discovery is the riskiest time to be safe. The desire to be safe will only neutralize your ability to take the necessary risks to discover who you are.

Once you make that initial step outside your comfort zone, expect the flood gates to open. Your life will begin to unfold in front of your eyes, and you'll continue to be excited for every new opportunity that comes your way. But to get to that point, there's work to be done, which is okay. Although it may seem difficult at first, your dedication will soon pay off.

There's so much more out there for you. *So much more.* Everything you've ever dreamed about is just over the edge of your comfort zone.

Do you trust yourself to cross that line?

> **TRUSTING YOURSELF IS THE FIRST STEP IN RECOGNIZING YOUR FULL POTENTIAL.**

#10 REJECT THE NORMAL

I think it's fair to agree that the desire to fit in is something everyone experiences at some point in their life. We yearn for acceptance. Not only for acceptance, but we want to shape our personalities and qualities around what we think other people would appreciate. Yet, this isn't how life should be. Sadly, whoever decided to start the rumor that fitting in was important really threw society for a whirlwind.

Too many people go through life stressed out and overwhelmed about their appearance, passions, purpose, and actions. When in actuality, we should have the confidence to be whoever we want to be and do whatever we want to do. But that's tough to do in a world full of judgment, competition, and comparison. So, what's the way around all this?

Reject the normal.

The most crucial step in our own growth and progression is trusting and believing that it's totally fine to do what *we* want to do and not what *others* think we should do. According to our society, this is sometimes looked down upon. Going against the grain is, well, a "Why the hell would you do that?" moment. It takes some serious brashness to be unique and evolve into an image *you* create and not what others create.

We need to overcome the false belief that we have to fit in with everyone around us. However, this will require us to go outside our comfort zone. That's another part of the challenge when you reject the normal. First, you have to understand everyone doesn't have to accept you, and then you have to hurdle outside your comfort zone to do something different.

Instead of searching for acceptance, search for genuine people. They will accept you for who you are. Those people are the ones that count. They value your unique but invaluable, self-built character. Their energy and acceptance will continue to motivate you to be who *you* want to be.

Rejecting the normal sets yourself up to a life worth living, as long as you reject the normal for the purposes of chasing a dream.

Let's put it this way: In 1929, a young boy, who eventually became the middle child, was born in Atlanta, Georgia. He came from what most would call a religious family. His grandfather was a minister in rural Georgia before moving to Atlanta to start the family in the late 1800s.

When his grandfather moved the family to Atlanta, he took it upon himself to rebuild the faith and energy of a small struggling church. With his pride, which runs in the blood of this family, he manifested this church into a powerful, faithful, and strong congregation. But all good stories come to an end. That young boy's grandfather passed away in 1931, leaving it to that young boy's father to take the church into his name. It was no surprise when he, too, became a name known by many in the community.

This was a family of power. But they seemed to always be the ones with fingers being pointed at them; they were called names and got the shortest end of the stick. They were a Black family and racism was a prominent issue in the everyday lives of many American citizens. The young boy's father tried everything he could to shield him from this racial prejudice, but it was close to impossible.

Fast forward a handful of years, this "young boy" became a man and was progressing rapidly. He had rejected his father's religious ways, but eventually regained his faith. Yet, that's beside the point. What matters in this story is his quality of activism. He had a powerful voice, presence, and, for his age, was advanced. By this time, he had already completed his Ph.D. and earned his degree. It was 1955, and he was 25 years old.

He met with many other activists because he wanted to make a change. He wanted to do something outside his comfort zone. He wanted to reject the normal.

He quickly gained national recognition. He was something new for our nation, and people believed we needed him because, well, we did. He was very much a proponent for non-violent protests. His approach was positive but different than usual. He didn't worry about what people thought of him because he knew his calling: to create unity.

In 1963 this man stood up to a podium and with pride and power said, "I have a dream, that my four children will one day live in a nation where they will not be judged by the color of their skin, but by the content of their character."

This man was Martin Luther King Jr., and he rejected the normal to chase a dream.

Not only is the story of Dr. King Jr. a reminder of our history, it's one of the best examples of rejecting the normal and living outside your comfort zone. Without that confidence, passion, and uniqueness, who knows where we would be today.

But let's focus on you, the one I'm writing this book for. If you want to get to a point in your life where you have the courage to reject the normal and the desire to live outside your comfort zone, there are a couple of things you need along the way.

First, you need faith. Faith in yourself, faith in your desires, faith in your uniqueness. Second, you need motivation, the almighty of doing anything uncomfortable, difficult, and challenging that's really going to put you to the test.

Unfortunately, motivation is one of the toughest things to come by. Sometimes it's almost impossible to spark. You see, motivation doesn't just happen. It's not going to appear at your front door one day yelling, "Hey buddy, get your life out the door. It's time to go for it." No, that's not how this shit works. If it did, oh man, life would be different.

Motivation comes from something else. It's created, not received. And who creates it? *You*. You must spark motivation through your own actions. You must *do* something to *feel* motivated. That's the approach you need to take when you want to reject the normal and stand for uniqueness. You must not only *feel* motivated, but you must *create* the motivation.

Next time you think of taking that first step outside your comfort zone, just step. I don't care if the step is one foot out the door or 10 feet down the street to your car so you can drive where you need to go. Just do it because you can. Once you take that first step, your path to rejecting the normal is history.

You'll be well ahead of most everyone around you because you made a decision to take the initial action. Everything after it will begin to fall into place. One stepping stone at a time. Your life will unfold like dominoes toppling over each other one after another after another.

When you find the power to create that motivation, you'll be able to run wild and have the courage to reject the normal. When you reject the normal, you set yourself apart from the masses.

That's a good thing, you should want that. If no one has paved a path that resonates with you, then go pave your own and inspire people with your confident leap of faith. When there's no one to inspire you, that just sets you up to find your own niche and serve as an inspiration for people to come after you.

However, let's cut to the real shit. The grass isn't always greener on the other side when you devote yourself to going against the grain. Sometimes (more like, a lot of the time) it's full of doubters, naysayers, skeptics, and pessimists. Not everyone is going to support you, and that's the damn truth. Alongside your motivation and inspiration, you're going to deal with loads of negativity. I mean, for God's sake, you're going against what people think you should do. That right there is an invitation for some serious haterade.

But, deflect all the negativity. People who feel the need to use their energy in a way to bring you down are usually envious of the qualities you possess to do something so "out there." When I see those people in my life, I sense jealousy. I use that to my advantage, though, because it's a sign I'm doing something right.

Not only that, but trust your gut. Trust yourself. You know what you want in life. Don't let the words of other people get in your head and shape your reality. Let *you* shape your reality. Do what you want to do. Choose how you want to live. Devote yourself to the things that matter to you. Remember to focus on you and not what others think you should be doing or who you should be.

Rejecting the normal isn't for everybody, but I believe it's for *you*. It's for the people who want to go after something worth their life. It's for the people who want to set themselves apart from the general population of our world. It's for the people who want to stand up for exactly what they want. It's for the people who want to devote themselves to living outside their comfort zone. True living exists in places of discomfort and challenge.

Do you want to be one of those people who live in their comfort zone? Or, do you want to feel like you are truly living? Are you ready to reject the normal and stand for uniqueness?

You have the power to make this decision and nobody can, or will, stop you. You have the courage to live outside the zone that society makes you believe you need to live within. You have the confidence to put down your foot and say you've had enough. If you don't believe it, then you'll have to use the trust you built within yourself and tell yourself you can. When you see your capabilities, you'll never look back at living a life like everyone else.

Go make this life yours.

> NOTHING HAPPENS WITHOUT ACTION.

#11
GIVE YOURSELF PERMISSION TO BE A BEGINNER

"You need to give yourself permission to be a beginner."

That's something my partner told me, and it changed everything for me. From that moment on, I gained a fresh perspective on how to approach new endeavors. It ultimately gave me the key to the gate of learning new crafts.

I believe that rejecting the normal is actually one of the easier parts of living outside your comfort zone. Yeah, it takes a load of courage and trust, but the real work begins after—when you're in the thick of it all. Most often, when we decide to reject the normal, we also devote ourselves to taking on something new. It's usually something we've never tried in our lives, or if we have tried, we can count the amount of times on one hand.

I think we can all agree that being a beginner at anything in life isn't where we all feel our most pride. We feel vulnerable. We feel isolated. We feel intimidated. We feel like it's easy to just give up because we still have one foot out the door. We feel as if everything in the world is against us and trying to keep us from achieving success in our latest venture. That's because it is.

The types of people who succeed at something brand new and get to a point of satisfaction or fulfillment are generally people who represent dedication, hard work, positive mindsets, and, most importantly, patience. It's never people who choose laziness over repeated hard work. It's never people who want instant gratification or, in better terms, people who aren't patient and want results instantly. You never see people who succeed at something new repeatedly tell themselves they can't do it.

Being a beginner is challenging, at the very least. It's uncomfortable and, by my standards, frightening. There's a high chance of failure. What's worse than that? I'm not sure. But, what I do know, and I try to keep this in mind often, is that if there's a high chance of failure, there's also a chance of breaking through the other side and achieving more than you imagine. High risk, high reward. Come on, you know the drill.

Once you've found the courage to reject the normal, stand for uniqueness, and pledge to live outside your comfort zone, it's time to accept being a beginner. Yet another challenging stepping stone in your journey of self-actualization. It's worth it, I swear. Each step along the way is a battle of its own. The truth is: without everything in between, you wouldn't be able to get to the end.

I was sitting in my apartment one evening questioning my life, a lot. I was writing and thinking about all the different avenues I want to go down before my time is up. I thought about how ever since I hopped on the creative train there had always been a feeling of something missing from my life. The good thing? I knew exactly what it was.

I was always envious of musicians. Not only because of the performing aspect, but because they create something that makes people connect with each other on a whole other level. I've always wanted to create and write music because I want people to feel emotions they've never felt before. I want to move people. That's the goal with all my work.

Music has always been the one missing puzzle piece in my life. For me, when I try something new (and choose to become a beginner), I have to submerge myself into that pond. There's no dipping my toes in, that just leaves room for me to come up with reasons why I'm "too late" or "too old" or "not good enough" or how it's "not meant to be." If I want to reject the normal and do something that may seem off my normal path, I have to put all my marbles into the process of learning.

So, without further ado, I dove into the pond purchasing everything I needed for a quick DIY home studio. Just enough to give me the encouragement to go for it. Ahh, fun shiny new toys. But, there was an issue. I had no clue what to do with any of it. I was legitimately confused. I was vulnerable and frightened. I was a beginner.

Just like most of us in a similar situation, I immediately began to question my decisions. Can I do this? Is it worth all the time? Are there too many people ahead of me? What if it doesn't pan out and it's all a waste? Are people going to judge me for doing something different? You know, the normal shit we ask ourselves every day.

Within the first couple days I was ready to quit. I came up with enough excuses as to why I shouldn't do it instead of reasons why I *could* do it. I was preparing to toss it all in the air and walk out the door. Call it a career! Less than a week was enough. I'd had it; it wasn't meant to be, and being a beginner was a load of bullshit.

When the irrational thinking concluded, I took a deep breath and went for a walk. I began to contemplate more. The same negative questions popped back in my head. I wished the right thoughts would just come up. You know, like the positive voice in my head I thought I had instilled for moments like this. Waiting and waiting, the doubt rose. I was just about ready to walk back home and sell everything when something came to mind.

I thought about when my time on this planet is up. I thought about how I would hate to have lived with any regrets. I knew that if I didn't give this whole music thing a go, it would slowly get to me. It would make me ask, "What if?" I never want to ask "What if?" in life. Whether I succeed or fail, I would much rather try so I can live without wondering what would have happened if I just went for it. So I agreed to keep with it and embrace the process.

After I went on my "searching-for-the-right-answers walk," my partner came through the door and saw me in contemplation. I explained there was only one thing in my life that's in my control to try that I haven't tried, but I was reluctant to go after it.

She looked at me and said, "You need to give yourself permission to be a beginner."

If I told you that one sentence didn't resonate with me more than anything I'd ever heard, I'd be the biggest bullshitter ever. It's so simple, yet one of the most profound pieces of advice I've ever received. You deserve to hear it too because it applies to all of us.

This is something I remind myself of every day. It's the sole thing that keeps me on track. It allows me to not fear my ambition, but to be more ambitious. It can do the same for you.

When you take on any new task, hobby, endeavor, or project, it's important to remember that accepting the fact that you're a beginner is okay. There's nothing wrong with it. The nice thing about being in that position is your growth potential—it's infinite. You're at the bottom; the only way for you to grow is toward your north star—the vision and dream you set your mind on.

The incremental progress along your path is the drug that keeps you going. Your incremental progress can serve as two things: 1) your motivation to keep striving for more and 2) small victories to celebrate. Truth be told, with those two things I believe you can be unstoppable. Not only will your progress feed your mindset to understand your potential, but it's going to make you feel damn good along the way. Of course, there will be hiccups, but those hiccups are just more opportunities to learn.

Take those bumps in your journey how you want, but I've found we can use them to our advantage to elevate our craft and advance quicker. If we let those lessons pass us without absorbing the information, then what's the point of wanting to get outside your comfort zone to do something new?

Become a receptor of everything around you when you're a beginner. Be like a sponge—absorb everything and anything surrounding you. Use your awareness to notice what you can capitalize on and what you can utilize to take yourself to the next level.

Start to believe that it's okay to be at rock bottom. You must realize that finding a new path at the base of the mountain isn't crazy, but rejuvenating. It's a decision you need to make to start something new, something that will challenge you to learn and develop a new skill set. When you're climbing, and it starts to get tough, remember that it's normal to be a beginner.

Don't overthink being a beginner. The negative voice in your head will try to get you to complicate everything along the way. It's going to make the smallest problems look like unrivaled beasts that can't be beat. But it's not the problem or situation that life presents that keeps you from moving forward, it's your mindset and thought process. Sometimes it's the pebble in your shoe that makes the mountain hard to climb.

> **THE INCREMENTAL PROGRESS ALONG YOUR PATH IS THE DRUG THAT KEEPS YOU GOING.**

#12
CURIOSITY OF EXPERIENCE

In 2019, I was interviewed on *Purpose in the Youth*, which is a podcast built around unfolding the stories of people who've found their passion. As the final question, I was asked to offer a parting piece of advice for people who want to set off on their own journey. Not only that, but also find their niche and go after it with passion. It was a question that didn't take much thought because it still holds true for me today. It's something I carry in my mental toolbox to help me grow into new areas of my own life. I think it can do the same for you.

My answer was (and still is), "Be curious. The curiosity of experience can lead to self-realization, and the quality of time spent in each of those experiences matters. Without curiosity, we will never learn what's out there for us to chase."

Curiosity is the catalyst to finding something new, energizing, and something you can be genuinely passionate about. But, without seeking those experiences, we are stuck with what we know. We are stuck with what we have, which, in the process of self-discovery, isn't what we want. Usually to discover our path, we must try anything and everything.

Even if you don't think it's something you'll find interest in, it's best to just roll the dice.

The curiosity of experience is something we all need to practice constantly. Whether you found a path that resonates or not, it's important to always be curious about new experiences. This allows our life to expand into new areas and helps us evolve into the multi-faceted individuals we were always meant to be.

However, to really tap into those facets, we need to experience as much as humanly possible. We need to put ourselves in both familiar and unfamiliar situations to discover our various talents. Get your hands a little dirty with something different. The worst that can happen is that you'll figure out you never want to have that experience again. But, if we don't put ourselves through that experience, we will live with the uncertainty of what would have happened if you just gave it a go.

Living in a bubble of "What if?" isn't worth it. It's a waste of your mental space and yields a potential for living in regret. It's much more worth it to seek out whatever is on your mind to get some answers. Living with regret isn't only a "Why would you want to do that?" kind of thing, it also doesn't make sense when you only have one shot here. You have one life. Do everything and anything you want to do in that one life because (for lack of a better way to say it) we're all going to eventually die. When we die, our opportunities shift, depending on your belief of what happens next.

But anyway, I believe we were supposed to be learning about the curiosity of experience. Yeah sure we could try something out for a day and say "Ehhh, not for me." But does that do us any good? No. We need to be more curious than that. And we need to get all the quality out of the experience that we can.

The longer you spend time with an experience, the more you'll begin to know. Sit with it, let it simmer, and see all sides of the experience. An experience should be three dimensional, if you will. Spend enough time to find out what you like, what you don't like, what about it makes you feel energized, and what about it makes you feel like you've had enough. I'm not a believer of making a rash, immediate decision when you try something completely new.

Not only is that an invalid decision in my mind, but you didn't give it time to evolve into anything. It's similar to the cliché, "Don't judge a book by its cover." Let's put it in terms that will make sense to both of us. Pretend we are strangers for the sake of this example.

We meet at a coffee shop while I'm getting my patriotic Americano (if you ever want to order me something, I'm all about that no-room-for-creamer type of coffee) and we chat for a bit. Imagine if I decided our connection wasn't worth my time in the first five or 10 minutes. Seems pretty unfair, at least in my eyes. Sounds like I'm doing two things: 1) judging a book, you, by its cover and 2) not focusing on the quality of time spent in that experience with you. Just so you know, I'd never do something like that. So please, still buy me a coffee if you'd like.

But the point is: deciding how you feel about someone or an experience in a short period of time isn't rational. Just as

I would give you my time of day and learn about your story, do the same for any new experience in your life. Go into that experience with the mindset of spending quality time with it. Be fully present because that's when you'll learn what you need to know, especially if it's something completely out of your comfort zone.

Experiences give us life. Without new experiences, we would all be bored as hell. I speak for myself, but if I'm not doing something, either new or old, I begin to question how I use my time. So I continue to seek new experiences and sit with them for as long as I need until I can make a rational decision on whether it is right for my life or not.

The curiosity of experience and the quality of time spent in those experiences is very similar to financial investing. There are many different approaches and tactics to investing, some work and some don't. But, as an investor, you'll never know what works until you try it. You can buy a ton of stocks and sell them quickly to make a quick buck, but that doesn't have the best long-term value. You could also buy the same amount of stocks and hold them for years until their value significantly increases, which is more in line with what we are talking about here.

Holding on to stocks or investments is closely related to spending quality time in your new and unfamiliar experiences. If you leave one foot out the door and bail too soon, it's likely you'll miss out on the full potential of your investment. If you don't sit with an experience long enough, it's likely you'll make an irrational decision and miss out on the potential of something that resonates outside your comfort zone.

Alongside giving yourself permission to be a beginner, curiosity is something we all need to possess to unlock our full potential. It's the one thing that motivates us to try something new and open the doors to something that's potentially life changing. Without it, we'll continue to sit on our asses and settle for what we have, even if it's something we don't want.

The harsh truth of our society is that too many of us decide we're okay with what we were handed. When in actuality, it's in our best interests to drop that notion and go after what we want.

It's common to have a fear of curiosity. I mean who the hell feels comfortable doing something completely new and random without knowing what the outcome will be. I'm no superhero. I was once in the same boat as you may be now. Scared shitless, I was about ready to settle for what I had—a lame office job, working for "the man," not receiving the recognition I deserved, feeling no fulfillment for what I was doing with my day, and dreading Mondays, Tuesdays, Wednesdays, Thursdays, and Fridays from 9 am to 5 pm.

Having a list of reasons why I wasn't appreciating my day was the catalyst to me overcoming my fear of being curious about what else is out there. It's common for us to stuff those things down—the harsh truths. It's common for us to avoid the shitty things we know about our current situation. But that doesn't mean it's wrong to accept them, recognize them, and change them. You don't have to live with what you're handed in life. You have the ability to choose to do anything you want.

Choose to be courageous. Choose to represent confidence. Choose to try new things. Choose to take on new responsibilities. Choose to seek the unfamiliar. Choose to realize that the outcome of your life is in your hands. Choose to take the appropriate steps to get outside your comfort zone. Choose to do something that will challenge you, bring in positive change, help you evolve into the person you were always meant to be—the best version of yourself. Choose to be curious.

Doing otherwise imposes a limitation that makes us believe what we know—what we were handed—is all we can achieve. Our potential is as big as our imagination. It's as big as we tell ourselves it is. If we settle for the experiences we currently have, especially the ones we loathe, then we're not pushing up against our boundaries. We are not knocking on the door of the next level—the level that you dream of.

Sure, you may feel like you want to take that with a grain of salt, but after you've done so, I suggest you reconsider your approach. Look through a new lens and drop your old habits. The new you is someone who embodies all the qualities represented within the curiosity of new experiences—courage, confidence, trust, ambition, motivation, and faith. With this mindset, you'll embrace this new found curiosity and take it with you wherever you go.

Next time you're sitting on your couch scrolling through Netflix and complaining about how unfortunate you are for what you were given in life, just stop. You can change the outcome of your life by seeking new experiences, managing the quality of those experiences by making them as three dimensional as possible, and learning more about what you're passionate about.

 The ball is always in your court if you want it to be, you just need to come to terms with yourself and agree that you have the power to do whatever you want to do. There's a whole new world within you, but you must excavate it.

 Stop wasting your time in front of the TV, or whatever you use as a distraction from the reality of life, and take action. Be excited about the unknown because it holds answers to your journey. Don't distract yourself from unlocking your full potential because then you're selling yourself short. That's bullshit. You deserve more.

 Pledge to give your own life an opportunity to flourish and radiate at its highest frequency. Break free of distractions that are holding you back from your own curiosity.

 Distractions will always be there, but your time won't.

> THE CURIOSITY OF EXPERIENCE CAN LEAD TO SELF-REALIZATION.

#13

COMPLACENCY: A TRUE SICKNESS

When something in our lives is comfortable, we are quick to feel satisfied and overly content—complacent. Whether it's fulfilling or not, comfort is something we all tend to seek. It's what keeps us somewhat sane, but it also keeps us somewhat stagnant. It's safe and toxic at the exact same time.

Our complacency is a headache of its own kind. It's hard to overcome because why would we want to change something if we feel satisfied? That feeling of content is just another way our ego tells us to stay put. It's another way for the voice in our head to tell us not to change anything because we're safe. Yeah sure we're safe, but are we pushing the limits beyond our comfort zones? No, not at all.

If I was a doctor, I would diagnose our society with a new kind of disease—a plague we've yet to learn about. It would be on the brink of becoming a pandemic, decided by yours truly, and impossible to heal with medication unless we all agreed that implementing a mindset shift and gaining a new perspective was medication.

I would diagnose our entire society with the *complacency plague*.

The flow of our lives naturally causes the complacency plague. We're all searching for something that allows us to fall into a groove, a defined path. However, many times that groove can take an unknown turn and we become so content with our safety that we are reluctant to introduce change.

When an unknown turn occurs and we can't make proper adjustments to counteract it, we allow the complacency plague to take over. Spreading like wildfire, we begin to succumb to feeling satisfied with what we currently have.

In our mind, satisfaction is a godsend, especially in a world that's constantly doing its best to make our lives more difficult. Well, it seems like a godsend, because satisfaction brings us a feeling of safety. However, this is our mind tricking us into thinking that we need to stay right where we are if we don't want things to go south. That's also the complacency plague doing its best to create limiting beliefs. We believe there's nowhere else we need to go, and we are right where we're supposed to be.

While that may be right in some cases, such as when you don't want to push your limits to unlock your full potential, most of the time complacency is a dangerous mindset to have. Complacency may make you feel pleasure, so you may ask, "Why would I consider pushing myself out of my comfort zone if I'm somewhat satisfied?"

Being too complacent has the potential to derail your personal progression and possibly even your career. When we are complacent, we refuse to work to improve. We are able to decide that what we have is good enough. The second we make that decision and come to those terms, we shut off an entire world of improvement. We build boundaries so high that escaping this complacency plague is nearly impossible.

If you stay within your complacency, you almost set yourself up for failure. Things in your life will remain the same, which makes you feel good about yourself, but everything outside your safety zone will continue to change. Everything in life will continue to grow, change, and develop, making what you have to offer obsolete. This quickly turns that safe complacency zone into a danger zone. You'll learn this isn't where you want to spend your life.

We could keep beating the complacency plague over the head with a hammer, but I'm not sure that would do us any good.

Now that we understand this new-age sickness—the complacency plague—there are a few things worth noting. First, you don't deserve this sickness because you have the power to make the proper changes. Second, you can only cure this with action and faith. And finally, it's probably a good idea to identify some signs that you're becoming complacent—that you're catching the plague:

1. YOU ARE NO LONGER STRIVING TO DO YOUR BEST (OR MORE)

Let's take a look at the average couch potato. That type of person is typically unmotivated, relaxed (not in a good way), and has surrendered to their current lifestyle. They have given up on all possibilities of striving to do their best, at least for the time being (until they read this book). Instead of choosing to strive for more in life, they choose to strive for more on Netflix. It's a backwards equation, but it's a real one.

I'm not saying if this description fits you that you're completely shit out of luck. What I'm saying is this is a common situation many of us fall into. We find something entertaining and let it distract us because it makes us happy enough. Well, guess what? "Happy enough" isn't going to cut it if you want to strive for things outside your comfort zone.

Don't be like the couch potato. Don't be like someone who doesn't want more. Be someone who is willing to stand up and put their best foot forward. Regardless of how much progress that step brings you, you're willing to take it because you know it's in the direction of trying to do your best.

2. YOU ARE NOT SEEKING NEW OPPORTUNITIES

I think it's safe to say a lot of us enjoy a routine. It gives us structure, keeps us in check, reduces the stress of our day and, for a lack of a better term, makes our life routine. I say this with confidence because I've been there: When things in life get comfortable and satisfying, we tend to not seek new opportunities because what we have is good enough. What we have brings us enough fulfillment that we don't feel like we need any newness.

However, this should be an immediate red flag. Well, it is for me, and I want to bring this up so it becomes a red flag for you. Seriously, SOS, we got an issue.

Sure, you can be content with what you have and not seek opportunities. That's fine, I'm not telling you that you can't do that. But, if you're on a mission to become the best version of yourself and truly expand into new areas of life, the word "settle" shouldn't be in your vocabulary.

If you want more—if you want to continually progress—you'll never be drawn to settling for what you have. You should have an appetite for opportunity. You should want progress like it's the thing that makes your heart beat. You should seek those new opportunities outside your comfort zone because you know it's going to take you to places you want to go.

Here, let me tell you how I view this in my own life. I live a life where I always want more. Now this doesn't mean I'm not satisfied or unfulfilled with what I currently have, but it does mean I know there's potential for new and greater opportunities outside my comfort zone that can unlock a new level of my potential. This kind of living isn't some gift I was blessed with. No, it's a decision. It's a choice to want more and want newness. You can make that choice, too.

3. YOU CHOOSE COMFORTABILITY OVER COURAGE

Comfortability is too warm and fuzzy to be something you should chase if you want to work to improve. It's the teddy bear we all had as a kid growing up; there for you when you need something to make you feel like everything is okay—safe. However, that comfort doesn't teach us much besides the fact that if you really want to fall back on something, you can. To me, comfort is like a participation trophy.

Participation trophies teach us that losing is okay by giving us an award for trying.

When I was 10 years old, I was playing on a superb baseball team that regularly won tournaments. But, much like a lot of things in life, just because you're at the top doesn't mean you'll stay there. We eventually lost and received participation trophy awards.

After the award ceremony, our coach made us all throw away those trophies in front of our parents. It was a lesson in exactly what we're talking about here, and it's a lesson I never let go of. This lesson thickened my skin and allowed me to understand that failure is real.

We need to learn that you won't always win, and when you lose, you're not rewarded. In other words, we need to learn that failure is going to happen, and we need to know how to remedy it. You shouldn't get a BS trophy with your name on it that says, "Nice try. You lost, but here's a warm, fuzzy piece of plastic to make you feel good about yourself." Instead, you should experience the feeling of failure. Because when you feel that, you'll be able to cultivate the courage to do whatever it is you're doing 10 times better to avoid failing again.

So, when you feel comfortable in your journey, take a step back. Analyze your situation and recognize the steps you need to take to escape your comfort zone before you fall into the downward spiral of complacency. Comfortability is good, sure, but is it really what makes us become the best versions of ourselves?

4. YOU ARE NOT BUILDING OR CULTIVATING NEW RELATIONSHIPS

One way to grow as an individual and strive toward new opportunities is by always wanting to expand your network. Believing you know everyone you need to know to become who you want to become is a fallacy. Your network is your net worth, and who you know *does* actually matter.

If you're living in a time where you believe everyone in your circle is the perfect combination of souls, I beg you to reconsider that thought. Sure, they might be amazing people who have taught you a lot to get you where you are. However, there's a ceiling of what they can teach you, help you with, and offer you. I'm not saying go dump all your current friends, that's not the point at all.

What I'm saying is this: If you're not building or cultivating new relationships, your complacency is making you believe the people you currently have is all you ever need. That belief is one of the biggest blocks in the pursuit of striving for more.

5. YOU RUN AWAY FROM THINGS THAT FEEL LIKE WORK

Most of the time, life outside our comfort zone is a challenge. It's difficult. It's not a cake walk. But that doesn't mean you should avoid it. I actually believe that if something isn't easy it means you *should* do it because the hard things in life are typically the most rewarding.

Which is more rewarding: flipping through the TV and successfully finding a good Netflix show (which I know can be hard)? Or, cultivating the courage to use your voice more, going after something that brings you to tears because it's so damn hard to achieve, putting every ounce of passion and love you have within your body into a piece of work, and going against the grain and taking a leap of faith outside your comfort zone to seize a dream you once thought was unattainable until you realize you have the power and strength to achieve literally anything?

Let's agree the laundry list above is much more rewarding. I say that with confidence because all of those things take hard work. There's nothing like completing something challenging and looking back to say, "I did that. It was my dedication and devotion to the grind that made me achieve it." It's an indescribable feeling when you give something every bit of energy you have and blow it out of the water.

But, it's safe to say all of us (myself included) tend to run away from things that feel like work. If it looks or sounds hard, get out of there. I'm kidding, don't do that, but that's how our brains are wired to react to tough situations.

We are designed to protect ourselves when we feel unsafe. We are programmed to take the easy route because we know we can't get hurt. But that's not going to bring you much besides continuing to stay complacent with your current situation.

If you have a mindset that perceives work as the worst thing humanly possible, it's safe to say I've just diagnosed you with the complacency plague. You're not alone, I've been there too, along with a ton of other people who are content with their current situation.

There was a time in my life where complacency was an everyday type of gig. I had been working in the mortgage industry for two years and my paychecks were looking mighty fine. I hadn't seen that kind of money my entire life. My bank account looked glamorous. But did I feel glamorous? Not even the slightest bit.

I remember thinking to myself that I had found my calling. Looking back, I laugh hysterically. The mortgage industry is the furthest thing from my calling. I was becoming complacent with my situation because I felt protected by my paycheck. However, I truly didn't feel happy about how I was spending my time. I discovered that working in the mortgage industry wasn't fulfilling my purpose of living a creative and adventurous life where I could encourage others to be the best version of themselves.

When I recognized I was settling for what I had because it made me feel safe and comfortable, I took a step back. I made a promise to myself that I would find something that brought me real joy. That decision changed the course of my life. I began to see my creative outlets as potential areas I could turn into a career. I started to discover the power of following your interests and letting your heart guide you.

Without trusting and following my interests, I wouldn't be writing this book, let alone be a writer. I'd be stuck working a job that didn't align with what I value most—creativity, adventure, and inspiring others to live a more meaningful life.

You have the opportunity to make a similar choice to live outside your comfort zone. But you must have the boldness to choose courage over complacency.

> **HAVE AN APPETITE FOR OPPORTUNITY.**

#14

GROWTH HACKING FAILURE

If there's one thing that makes every one of us uncomfortable, it's experiencing failure. Try and think about the last time you felt genuinely good about failing. Right, probably never, which is understandable. Not only does failure strip us of achieving something we desire, but it also strips us of our pride. It leaves us in one of the most vulnerable states we can experience—weak, uncertain, and frightened to make any sudden movements toward achieving another goal.

Come on, you know exactly what I'm talking about. You decide to go after one of your biggest dreams. You drop everything, and you legitimately give it everything you have. No more Netflix (ouch). No more doing a little work here and a little work there. No more half-assing. You pour every ounce of passion, determination, and belief into achieving the goal. But, as the story goes, you fall short. You weren't good enough, yet. And now you must sit there and sulk in that shitty feeling. We've been there. *All of us.*

But failure doesn't have to be like that, failure doesn't have to be something you view as a negative. There's potential for failure to be a net positive. Yes, I said positive. You can actually use failure to your advantage and let it propel you forward in your journey. Sound surprising? Well, let me tell you how you can do this in your life.

I've failed several times in the past and I know I'll fail several times in the future. It's inevitable, not only in my life, but yours too (sorry to break the news). Now, I haven't always had a healthy relationship with failing to be completely honest, and that's okay. However, I've worked tirelessly to embrace my failures and search for ways I can use them to benefit me.

Over the course of years, I've developed a system to help me extract the positives when I come up short. This system has stripped me of the fear of failure because I've set myself up with the resources I need to not let any failure set me back. This system can do the same for you.

Meet *growth hacking failure*. Growth hacking failure does not require new technical skills, superpowers, or years of experience. I've already done the legwork for you so you could benefit from a failure-proof system. All it requires of you is your mindset and, of course, the willingness to exist outside your comfort zone.

Growth hacking failure is built on three principles. First, switch the lens you see failure through. Second, don't take it personally. Third, uncover your lesson and adjust. Is it really that simple? Yes. Have most people overcomplicated dancing with moments of failure? Absolutely. Can failure result in growth spurts? 110%. So, although failure is far outside of most people's comfort zones, you can use this system as a tool to put your failures on your side. Let's dive into the three principles of growth hacking failure:

1. SWITCH THE LENS YOU SEE FAILURE THROUGH

Failure sucks when you see it as a negative. It eats you alive, pushes you backward on your journey, and sometimes even keeps you from chasing your wildest dreams. It's a wild beast, but luckily there are ways you can tame it.

The first step in growth hacking failure is making a conscious effort to shift your mindset around it. You need to decide that you will look at failure through a new lens and embrace a new perspective. Sure, failure can be devastating and unencouraging, but truthfully, it's only such if you believe it to be. Failure brings lessons, it brings eye-opening experiences and epiphanies, and it brings the resources you need to continue down your path and thrive outside your comfort zone.

What I am saying is this: As soon as you choose to view failure as a positive, you will experience its plethora of gifts. It's easy (and common) to think of failure and immediately have a sour taste in your mouth. But right now marks the end of that in your life. It's time you switch the lens you see failure through. It's time for failure to no longer stop you in your tracks and instead, push you forward. Don't worry about failure stealing your life force; it's there to teach you what you need to know to continuously grow.

2. DON'T TAKE FAILURE PERSONALLY

When you come up short, it's easy to stuff your mind with negative and self-sabotaging thoughts. *I'm not good enough. I'm a piece of shit. I'll never be successful.* These thoughts are dangerous, and they'll quickly take over your life and rip your vitality out of your hands.

It's crucial to deliberately choose to not let failure impact you on a personal level. You must remove your ego from a moment of failure and not beat yourself up over it. What's done is done. Dwelling on it and hitting yourself over your head is not going to do you any good. Don't waste your energy with that BS.

If you come up short, give yourself a few minutes to blow some steam off, but that's it. As a matter of fact, Tiger Woods has a 10-step rule in golf. If he hits a bad shot and fails at the tee box, he gives himself 10 steps to be upset about it, then he moves on. He doesn't let his failure steal his energy because he knows it's more sacred than that. He recognizes what happened, makes any adjustments needed, and moves forward. So, give yourself a few minutes or walk 10 steps, but after that, don't take it personally. Don't let it consume you.

Failure happens to all of us. You're not the only person that goes through this uncomfortable part of life. When it happens, *it's okay*. Don't beat yourself up. Don't feed your mind negative thoughts, and don't let failure derail you from your path. Take your 10 steps and look for the lesson.

3. UNCOVER YOUR LESSON AND ADJUST

If you can switch your perspective on failure and not take it personally, you'll find that there are life-changing lessons in a moment where you come up short. That's the secret to failure; if you can uncover your lesson and adjust, you'll be able to use that knowledge to help you progress on your journey and avoid making a similar mistake moving forward.

Failure is the teacher we never wanted but always needed. It might push you to the ground, but if you're willing to look for the lesson or for an opportunity to improve, it will lift you up. Oddly enough, the more you fail, the more you learn, and the more you learn, the more you grow.

Now is it all starting to make sense? Do you see how society has tricked you into believing that failure should be one of your biggest fears? The fear that holds you back from growing into the best version of yourself and discovering who you were always meant to be?

I'm here to teach you that failure can be on your side if you want it to be. If you growth hack failure, you can let it serve *you* instead of you serving it.

Failing doesn't have to be a permanent setback. Yeah, it might stop you in your tracks, make you feel like you've run into a giant brick wall that will never let you move forward, and completely tear you apart, but that's normal, expect that. However, it's temporary. Let it be temporary.

Failure makes you feel shitty, we all know that. But let it fuel you. Allow it to give you the motivation to go back and try 10 times harder. Give it the chance to serve you in ways you never knew failure could serve.

When you ask the general population about their take on failure, most people will probably say something along the lines of how failure kept them from chasing their dreams. But the truth is, the only reason why it's blocking those people is because they told themselves they couldn't overcome their failure. They believed that failure was a permanent setback. You don't have to be one of those people. You can be the person that says, "I tried, and I failed, and that's why I am successful."

Recognize that growth hacking failure is the quickest way to turn failure into a positive. Although failure is something that will always be out of your comfort zone, if you practice this mindset, it can help you discover more about yourself and what you need to know to become the best version of yourself.

Are you ready to embrace failure?

> **THE MORE YOU FAIL, THE MORE YOU LEARN, AND THE MORE YOU LEARN, THE MORE YOU GROW.**

#15 SEPARATE YOURSELF FROM FAMILIARITY

To put the icing on the cake and the cherry on the top, the quickest way to get out of your comfort zone and learn about yourself is by going rogue. Isolate yourself to the max. Remove all the unnecessary external forces from your life so you can focus on your own shit. Put yourself in a situation that sets you up for a crash course on life where you're the only student.

Ahhh, it was the olden days and the year was 2016. Just kidding, I remember it like it was yesterday because it pretty much was yesterday. But, to give me the benefit of the doubt, when my kids read this book in *many* future years, 2016 is going to sound like light years ago. Anyway, I'm 21 years old at the time and graduating college with a degree in finance. I didn't know what was about to come.

The world around me told me to start flinging my resume out to financial firms and hedge funds. Society made me think it was time to go from the classroom to a dull, gray, and unimaginative office. But I knew this was bullshit. I had the rest of my life to figure that out. I didn't see the point of jumping right into something most everyone sees as the next step after college.

Luckily, I had parents and siblings who encouraged the exact opposite. As the youngest of four, I watched each of my older siblings take advantage of a gap year—or gap months, if you will. So, for me, that always was the norm. I truthfully never had endeavors of landing a flashy job title and sexy paycheck right out of college. The golden handcuffs weren't something I envied, not then, and not now.

But, I knew that anything other than that was going to involve me getting outside my comfort zone. As a young adult who wasn't the most confident individual, taking some time off was nerve wracking. However, in my mind and my parents', it was apparent it was the next best step to build my character. There was an emphasis put on building your character instead of your bank account after college in my family, and that's something I will never let go of. I'll hold onto that lesson for future generations.

I embraced that mindset and chose to leave the country on a solo trip around Europe for three months. In other words, I decided that isolating myself from what I understood as normal and safe was the quickest way to get the furthest away from my comfort zone. This was the most influential decision of my entire life.

There was my life before this choice, and there was my life after—same person, two completely different lives and perception of who I was always meant to be.

This was my first experience with living outside my comfort zone. It was the first time in my entire life that I can say

I did something daring, something that made me feel utterly vulnerable. It stripped me of everything that made me feel safe and threw me out to figure some of my own shit out. It put me in life's crash course, and I had three months to try and graduate with summa cum laude.

It taught me how to drop all the negative self-limiting beliefs I had cultivated over the last handful of years. It forced me to put myself in social situations that I otherwise would have avoided. Each day was a new word problem, and I had 24 hours to solve it. Every solution had two things in common: confidence and intention. Without confidence and intention, this solo trip would have evolved into my quickest failure to date.

But luckily it didn't pan out like that. I told myself there was no other option besides extracting the most possible value from these three months of my life. It was one of those, "It's going to work because it has to or else I'm shit out of luck" moments of my life. I was obviously ready to make some changes in my life, and the only way to do that (in my mind) was by separating myself from my bubble. This was the most direct way for me to learn about who I genuinely wanted to be and the things in life I wanted to stand for.

By removing myself from a space of familiarity and challenging myself to branch out, I learned three things: 1) anything is possible if you trust yourself, 2) learning about yourself on a deeper level is one of the most exciting things in life and 3) everything in life begins to flourish outside our comfort zones, that's where the magic happens.

YOU DESERVE THIS SHIT

Now, I'm not saying everyone should drop what they're doing and run away to another country. Although it worked for me, you must find something that resonates with you. It must be something you can put some intention behind, because that's what we need when we are becoming the best versions of ourselves—intention, a shit ton of it.

What I'm saying is separating yourself from familiarity for a period of time is going to put you furthest away from your comfort zone. If you are truly determined and motivated to learn about yourself in the deepest way possible, this is what you need to put into your life's agenda. There's no time for questioning. Stop doing all the things that make you feel fuzzy and warm. Set yourself up to be in a position that's uncharacteristic of your typical patterns.

Whatever it is you decide to do, a lot of people will most likely label you "crazy" or say your decision is "irrational." But, in the nicest possible way, forget those comments. The negativity from others is an indicator that you're doing something right. It demonstrates that other people wish they had the same level of audacity and courage as you. But they don't, so instead, they will spend their time and energy trying to take you down. They don't want you to succeed.

Let their negativity be an extra kick in the ass and a couple ounces of fuel. Use that as inspiration and prove every single one of those negative comments wrong, and do it with pride. You're capable of doing something out-of-the-box, but expect other people to find your choice different. That's inevitable.

When you find your thing that's going to kick you out of your comfort zone, pledge to be a student to it for as long as you need. Hit the books, study, be aware of everything surrounding you, and, most importantly, enjoy the course. Even though this isn't a mandatory class, it's one you're deciding to enroll in because you know the best thing in life is to be happy with your own.

99

THE BEST THING IN LIFE IS TO BE HAPPY WITH YOUR OWN.

#16 COMFORT ZONES: WHAT YOU CAN DO WITH THESE LESSONS

We packed a lot of lessons and information in this section about not only comfort zones, but also how you can leverage living outside of them. I find this is one of the most talked about aspects of life, yet it seems to be the most challenging to embrace. Who in their right mind would want to choose being somewhere unfamiliar? It took me years to accept this and to live outside my comfort zone.

However, from the lessons I covered in this section, I've been able to learn to be comfortable with being uncomfortable. Truthfully, it's become a space where I prefer to live in. I know life outside my comfort zone is where I'll be able to follow my interests and learn the lessons I need to take my life to the next level.

I want you to feel the same. I want you to crave living outside your comfort zone like your life depends on it. In this chapter, I will help you do that. We will go over steps that can help you immediately take action on living outside your comfort zone. These steps will take courage, confidence, and trust, but I assure you they will benefit you and rocket launch you along your journey. These steps are choices that you can make on your own to design a new way of living:

1. **Build trust with yourself:** You are your own biggest critic, which sometimes makes it challenging to do something audacious—like living outside your comfort zone. You must build trust within yourself first before you're ready to live outside your comfort zone.

    To do so, you need to fill your mind with positive self-talk. It's as simple as that. Tell yourself "I can and I will." Feed your brain the mental nutrition it needs to realize that you're not only in control of your destiny, but you trust yourself to stand for uniqueness. (Chapter 9)

2. **Stand for the things you want in life:** Grasp the understanding that you need to live the life that *you* want and not how others think you should live. I've come to realize sometimes that in order to do that, you must reject what people perceive as "normal." You need to stand for anything you desire and want to chase, whether other people accept you for it or not. Don't search for acceptance. Surround yourself with genuine

people who support your journey, they will accept you for who you are. (Chapter 10)

3. **Be okay with being a beginner:** Don't get me wrong, being a beginner is never an easy situation. We're our own biggest critics, and this is the easiest way to beat ourselves up—by simply not being skilled at something we aspire to do well.

   However, you must realize that being a beginner is part of learning anything new. It's integral to gaining the skills you need to take a craft, hobby, or passion to where you envision it to go.

   Give yourself permission to be a beginner and begin to understand that it's in those moments you'll learn skills that will help shape your path. (Chapter 11)

4. **Be curious:** The curiosity of experience can lead to self-realization. Once I learned that, it was game over.

   Curiosity is innate within all of us. However, it's been trained out of us since a young age. As kids, we're at a curious high—we explore everything and experiment with our environment. But as we get older, it's looked down upon to try something new or different because you may fail, and for God's sake, failure is "bad."

   Forget about what society has made you believe. Embrace your inner child—your original or true self—and use your curiosity to your advantage. It changed my life, and it can change yours, too. (Chapter 12)

5. **Beware of your complacency:** It's easy for us to feel overly content when we are in a comfortable place

in our life. We want to sit back, relax, and coast. However, like me, you should do the exact opposite of that. Your complacency is a sickness, and you need to become aware of it.

If you aren't striving to do your best, are avoiding being courageous, or you run away from things that feel like work, it's likely you've been plagued by complacency. Good thing it's curable. How? By choosing to be courageous. (Chapter 13)

6. **Use failure to grow:** Up until now, you've probably seen failure as a negative. However, with a simple mindset shift, you can leverage failure and use it to help you grow. Remember to see it as an opportunity to learn a lesson that will help you get to your next stepping stone. Failure is your teammate if you're willing to lean into it. (Chapter 14)

7. **Separate yourself from familiarity:** The quickest way to get outside your comfort zone is by isolating yourself from what you feel is familiar. For me, that was going on a solo backpacking trip to Europe. For you, it may be different. But whatever it is, removing yourself from your typical and normal surroundings will jumpstart your journey outside your comfort zone. (Chapter 15)

While these seven action items and living outside your comfort zone may be daunting, I can tell you one thing: it's worth it. You'll never regret it, and you won't want to go back to choosing comfort. I haven't looked back once. After my first taste of what was outside my comfort zone, I saw a glimpse of the life I always wanted to live. You have the power and opportunity to feel the same way. You need to choose to be courageous and trust yourself that you're capable of doing this. You deserve this shit.

"

THE TRUE SENSE
OF LIVING EXISTS
IN PLACES OF
DISCOMFORT.

PART III
INTENTIONAL LIVING

Make conscious efforts to live aligned with your truest values and beliefs. Your decisions define you. Choosing a life that matters is completely in your hands.

#17
WHAT YOU'LL LEARN ABOUT INTENTIONAL LIVING

Do you want to make impactful decisions in your life that revolve around your beliefs and values? If you answered yes, then choose to lead a life of intentional living.

Intentional living consists of making choices that keep you connected with your life values. Choosing to live intentionally is a decision, it's a commitment, it's a promise you need to make with yourself. The decisions you make on a daily basis define you now and will define your future. With that in mind, this means you're able to choose a life that matters—one that *you* want to lead.

Living intentionally doesn't need to be complicated. It will only become complicated if you make it so. Instead, let go of doing it perfectly, stop overthinking, and trust your gut. Make decisions that feel right, the ones that represent the person you want to be or become. You can do it, trust me.

The goal of this section is to teach you how intentional living is an important puzzle piece to becoming the best version of yourself. It will demonstrate how this is a choice we can make to help our journey. Intentional living can move mountains, but only if you're willing to put forth conscious effort to implement it into your everyday life.

It's not rocket science, it's as simple as choosing to do things that aid your personal growth and support you as you progress further down your life path. It's your avenue to creating a life that aligns best with your view of how you want to live. Your choices empower you, don't give that up.

In this section, we'll talk about several different aspects of life that revolve around your decisions and the way you choose to do different things. It's frightening how much your decisions and choices can dictate your life, but it's true, and I believe that alone is a good enough reason to live intentionally. Think of it this way: Your choices can be the building blocks to not only your foundation but also the kingdom you build on top of that foundation.

The lessons in the following chapters, listed below, can spark a new flame in your life, and I'm excited to see how long that flame will burn:

- **Forming a routine**
- **The power of positive thinking**
- **How your network can elevate your life**
- **The importance of choosing your lifestyle**
- **Building a system to support your goals**
- **How your life is only as big as your aspirations**

It's safe to say that living intentionally isn't necessarily automatic, or something we do without conscious effort. For a period of time in my life I was far from intentional. I made decisions in spite of how I truly wanted to live. Instead, my decisions were influenced by how people would judge me and perceive who I was. I cared too much about what other people thought of me and not enough about how I felt on the inside—how my heart felt. This is when I had it all backwards.

Putting others before your heart is a recipe for a disaster. To remedy this situation, I pledged to make choices based on what aligned with my values and beliefs and not the values and beliefs of others. This changed everything and put me in the position today of being able to strategize my decisions in a way that helps push me further along in my journey. You can experience this, too.

Although intentional living may sound challenging, it doesn't have to be. Leave your old patterns behind you and step into a new version of you—the best version of yourself. Become conscious in your decision making and begin to understand that you can shape your life's arc through intentional living. Your conscious attempts to live a life that revolves around your values and beliefs will put you in the best position possible to unlock your greatest potential, create your identity, and become the best version of yourself.

#18
THE POWER OF ROUTINE

I'm a total morning guy, but that doesn't mean I always have been. Many people are morning people, but many others are not. A simple morning routine can boost your productivity. Studies indicate that when we are low on energy and our self-control is depleted, motivation goes out the window, which makes it hard to focus on tasks and execute to completion.

An energizing morning routine can have a large positive impact on your attitude, energy levels, and performance throughout the rest of your day. You're in control of winning your day before it even takes place. The way you move through the morning sets the tone for the rest of your day. So, why wouldn't you want to set yourself up for success?

Over time, and through finding a morning routine that works for me, I've come to the conclusion that my day seems scattered without a morning routine. My personal routine is there to let me know that every day will begin the same. This allows me to choose the tone for my day, set intentions, and complete some tasks early on, which gives me the confidence to complete more tasks throughout my day. The compound effect—small things done repeatedly become something greater—will be your friend.

For instance, making the bed. This is one of the most overlooked, yet easiest ways to start your day and set yourself up for more success. Sure, it's a small and seemingly insignificant thing to do, but its ripple effect is incomparable.

When you complete one task, it will compound into another task, and another task, and another task. Before you know it, by making your bed, which doesn't have to be an extravagant process (it takes me less than two minutes), you have motivated yourself to complete a handful of other tasks. To check off multiple tasks or to-do list items for your day, you must start with one task, so why not make it your bed?

When I first tried this "waking up early" thing, it wasn't pretty (to say the least). The moment I tried to get out of bed while the sun was still rising was about the time I thought I was trying to scale the face of Mount Everest. I'd slap the side of my face, rub my eyes, and slam my head back down into my plush pillows that somehow had a tether around me that kept me from starting my day. It was very much a push and pull, love-hate relationship I had with waking up early (at first).

Within seconds of my feet hitting the floor beside my bed I'd ask myself, "Where's my coffee?" A question that's, oddly enough, innate in many of us, and I'm sure we can all agree on that without debate. When I first started waking up early, you could expect me to jump right over to the coffee machine in the kitchen and throw the boldest, most caffeinated grounds into the machine to whip up the day's first cup. But, with time and repetition, waking up early got easier and easier, which meant less and less coffee.

Of course, if mornings aren't in your normal realm of living, it's going to be tough at first to implement that new pattern into your life. But that doesn't mean it's impossible. I found it easier to get used to by giving my morning somewhat of a schedule.

Instead of waking up and floating freely around the house, I created a structure that helps me start my day with productivity and intention. Here's an example of my morning routine:

1. EXERCISE

My first order of action is to get my blood flowing. I usually spend between 45 minutes to one hour exercising to start my day. I found this amount of time to work best for me, but it's important to find what fits into your schedule and what ultimately makes you feel good. Exercise can be anything that involves movement—yoga, running, dancing, lifting weights, boxing, Pilates. Find your niche.

Do something that makes you happy so you'll want to do it again, and again, and again. Sustainability is important, and the only way to sustain anything in life is by devoting yourself to things that you love, enjoy, and are wholeheartedly passionate about.

2. MAKE MY BED

My first real task of the day is making my bed, for reasons you are familiar with now that we have already touched on them. But it's worth reiterating. Completing an easy task early on in your day jumpstarts the compound effect, which is that every small thing compounds to something greater.

Not only that, but coming home to a freshly made bed is hands down one of the most underrated parts of the day. If your day was a wash, I guarantee you'll find gratitude in coming home to your sheets tucked, comforter straightened, and pillows upright. If not, we should have a conversation about finding appreciation in the smallest things in life.

3. MEDITATE

Quieting your mind before a long day of hard work is a necessity. I sit with my eyes shut for 15 minutes every morning, which helps me start my day with a clear mind. A lot of the time, we find what we are looking for where we don't want to look. And often, we don't want to look inside. I've found that closing your eyes is one of the easiest ways to open your mind.

4. JOURNAL

Journaling is my bread and butter. I start a new journal every year, so I have an archive that represents my mind and thoughts over the years. Journaling in the morning (and at night if you prefer both) doesn't have to take a large chunk of time. I spend less than five minutes writing five things I'm grateful for, my life purpose, and a positive affirmation. Although it's quick, it teaches me how to look at my life through an optimistic lens and brings forward things that I appreciate. It's a refreshing way to start my day and without it, I feel naked.

5. MAKE COFFEE

Halle-frickin-lujah! We made it. Who doesn't love a good cup of coffee to start the day? I think we can agree that most people already include this in their morning routine. Whether you prefer coffee, tea, or hot lemon water, get after it. I'm all about the caffeine, especially because I enjoy mixing in some functional mushrooms to kick start my brain for a full day of creativity.

6. FREE WRITE

Before I start my workday, I make sure the last thing I do is something that's fully focused on bettering myself and my craft. Most of the time, that's free writing. The nice thing about free writing is it can be anything I want to work on at the moment—mini essays, a book, or a story. It's my way of tapping into and unlocking my creative brain early on in the day.

However, free writing isn't for everyone. I'm a writer by trade, so it resonates. You, on the other hand, may have no desire to become a writer, and that's completely okay. This part of a morning routine can either be removed from your routine or you can replace it with a project or personal task you've been working on—poetry, meal prep, organizing an area of your house, or even spending time with your significant other or roommates.

Regardless of what you choose, it's important to find "me time." Put an emphasis on yourself and the work it takes to improve your life. Make personal growth a priority. You deserve this shit.

Now, you could complain that I didn't teach you how to make your own routine and instead told you how I spend my mornings, but let's not do that. Sometimes the best way to create something for yourself is to learn what works for others. Beyond sharing how I spend my time every morning, there are a few things I didn't mention that are the foundation of any successful morning routine.

Regardless of what you include and don't include, developing any type of morning routine involves similar guidelines—rules to follow, if you will. There's no point in blindly throwing together some stuff and hoping for the best. I think it's safe to say some sort of guide would be helpful in a situation like this, so without further ado, here are crucial tips for creating a purposeful and intentional morning routine:

1. SET BARRIERS AND BOUNDARIES

On your first go around, it may be challenging to separate yourself from your social life or interacting with other people in your household during the morning. I know from personal experience, it's extremely easy to get distracted in the morning and make excuses to not follow through with a morning routine. So you need to set barriers and boundaries. Make it known that for whatever amount you require, an hour or two or whatever it is, you need that time to yourself.

You have 24 hours in your day, I think it's safe to say that one or two hours to yourself isn't going to kill anyone. So, tell people around the house that you'll be MIA for a bit. Undivided attention is going to become your best friend if you truly want your morning to be intentional.

2. TURN OFF YOUR PHONE

This definitely goes hand in hand with creating boundaries. Shut your phone off or put it somewhere far, far away. In an age of social media, one of the easiest ways to become distracted and not follow through with a task is by keeping that bright lit screen directly in front of your face. The stimulus and dopamine you'll receive from your device is going to make you believe your morning routine can wait. Not today, sorry.

Your time is precious, and your Instagram feed isn't going anywhere (for now), so take a few hours without your phone. I guarantee you if you're able to separate from electronic devices for just a few hours, you'll see how much we let them consume not only us, but our entire day.

3. TAKE ADVANTAGE OF RITUALS

Include at least one ritual-like event in your morning routine. That can be brewing a cup of coffee, steeping your favorite tea, meditating, repeating affirmations to yourself in the mirror, or anything that feels ceremony-like to you. Rituals always have more importance to us than our day-to-day motions. By taking advantage of rituals, you can create a morning routine that slowly becomes your religion. It will be something you attend every morning.

Soon enough, once you get into the swing of things, you'll realize that your entire morning routine is going to become one wholesome ritual. The things that make up that routine will merge together until that ritual is one of the most sacred in your life. And the best part about it, this ritual belongs to you. It's for you and only you, and you're capable of bending it in any direction you wish to receive the most benefit from it.

4. BE CONSISTENT

Consistency is tough, don't get me wrong. There are some days I want to take off or accept defeat against my sorry excuses. We all have those days. Whether I feel a bit more tired than usual, or just lazy, it always seems I can find a reason why it's okay to take a day off. But I remind myself that the best hack for implementing something new in life is consistency.

Repeated action creates an atmosphere full of habits. So, when you're getting started, recognize the thoughts that make you believe it's okay to take a day off, then tell them to get out. Through consistency, you'll build a system that helps you achieve your goal of following through with a purposeful and intentional morning routine every single day.

Awesome, now you know everything there's to know. Just kidding. But you know enough to begin creating your own routine. There will always be more things to learn, but these four tips can create a strong foundation to help build your newest morning routine. Build your system and try it out until it breaks. Find the kinks, iron them out, and improve your efficiency. The best way to learn is by doing, and the best way to improve on anything is by taking those lessons and using them to refine your craft.

> "
A SIMPLE MORNING ROUTINE LETS YOU WIN YOUR DAY BEFORE IT EVEN TAKES PLACE.

#19
THOUGHTS ARE ENERGY

We live in an age where positive thinking is pushed more than the importance of your daily water intake. Now let's set this straight, I don't think it's honest to be positive 24 hours around the clock. That's not sustainable or even close to realistic. Life sucks sometimes, and we can't deny that. However, I believe that positive thinking can play a remarkable role in the fruition of your life, ideas, and dreams. Your mindset matters, and it can be a crucial building block of the path to becoming the best version of you.

I once heard someone say, "Your thoughts are energy, and your intentions create your reality." I wish I could give credit where credit is due, but their name has left my memory bank. Regardless, I want to include it in this book and, more importantly, this chapter.

Be cognizant of your thoughts. The power of thought is one of the most amazing tools we all possess. If you can think of it, you can visualize it. If you can visualize it, you can recognize the work that you need to act on to bring it into your reality. Emphasis on the word "work" because things in life don't just magically unfold unless you do something about it. As Jim Carrey says, "Visualization works if you work hard. That's the thing. You can't just visualize and go eat a sandwich."

The law of attraction is real. Simply stated, the law of attraction is the belief that positive or negative thoughts bring positive or negative experiences into a person's life. It's in our power to dictate the ecosystem we live in, and it all comes down to how we approach our thoughts every day. Sure, negative thoughts are sometimes hard to avoid because of the constant social pressure we all endure in our lives. But there's a path to recovery for all my negative thinkers out there.

It's safe to say that I also had patterns of negative thinking in my life. And now looking back on those times, I see why nothing was flourishing for me. I wasn't attracting much good in my life, and now I get it. This didn't change for me until I realized that the law of attraction involves living intentionally. It involves using the power of your mind and thought to help you understand what you want to attract.

But here's the real problem, there are a ton of people who preach positive thinking, which is good and bad. It's good because we need those people and it's always nice to have that reminder as we coast through life. However, it's bad because a lot of the time no one really teaches you how to get there. Everyone just assumes you'll get it, that it will just click and make sense. The reality is that's false (for most).

I believe in guiding and teaching individuals so they can implement new things into their life that will actually create positive change. I believe we're all here to learn things that will allow us to be the best version of ourselves. And if I don't teach you, or if we don't all teach each other what we know, then we are leaving a wealth of knowledge on the table. We don't deserve that wasted energy, we deserve to learn as much as humanly possible that will help us elevate individually (and collectively).

With all that being said, it's only fair to show you the six powerful steps you can use to change the course of your thoughts from negative to positive:

1. START THE DAY WITH POSITIVE AFFIRMATIONS

Positive affirmations are statements designed to help overcome negative thoughts, such as self-doubt, lack of confidence, and self-labeling. Through repetition, they can help improve your mental health and outlook on life. And the best thing is you can use them for all types of situations—work, stress, anxiety, success. Whatever it is you may have negative thoughts around, there's a way to excavate the positive side.

Personally, I write my positive affirmations in a journal, but it's important to create a system that works well for you. Whether that's repeating them out loud while looking in a mirror or writing them down on paper, you'll find it beneficial almost immediately. Before I forget to mention, these statements don't need to be intricate or difficult to come up with. Let them be as simple as, "I am worthy," "I am confident and successful," or "I am capable of achieving my dreams." Let simplicity surprise you with its power.

Think of it like going to the gym and tossing some iron around—the more you do it, the more natural it becomes. The more you repeat positive affirmations—positive statements—the more likely it is for your brain to think that way all around the clock. Treat your mind like a muscle; repeating positive affirmations can help create a muscle memory reaction. The continued repetition will guide you down a path that takes you further and further away from your unwanted patterns of negative thinking.

2. FIND GRATITUDE IN EVERY SITUATION

One of the drivers of positive thoughts and positive living is the ability to express and feel gratitude. Gratitude is simply being thankful for something or someone in your surrounding life. Similar to atoms and their relation to the foundation of everything we know, gratitude is the building block of positive thinking. Of course it's tough to find gratitude all the time because we live in a world that's inflated with a lot of negativity, but when you feel gratitude for the first time, you'll never want to let go.

The chills that run down your spine, the energy and flames that spark within, the wave of positivity you feel that ripples throughout your body is like nothing else. It's not only going to change your life and your mindset, but it will impact others. Gratitude is one of the most infectious, intangible things in life, and we all have the ability to spread that feeling.

If your $5 cup of coffee was a bit more bitter than it was the day before, be grateful that you even had the opportunity to have not one, but two cups. If your car's air conditioning isn't as cold as you wished on a summer day, be grateful you have access to a moving vehicle. If your food isn't cooked as you typically enjoy or your local grocery store is out of your favorite comfort food, be grateful there's food for you to eat. Oh, and don't forget about your heart, hands, limbs, brain, and ability to think thoughts and ideas. That matters too.

3. TURN FAILURES INTO LESSONS

I don't completely believe in failure the way most people do. It seems that many people think once you fail, you're out of luck. However, within every failure, there's at least one lesson—one that can be life changing. It's easy to immediately drown in a pool of negativity if we fail. We will quickly spiral down and nothing great will come of it.

If we can flip on the switch in our brains that tells us to extract a lesson from a failure, then we can use positivity as a rebuttal against negative thinking. Once I began practicing this anytime I failed (because I fail often), many areas of my life shifted drastically. I was surprisingly no longer scared to fail because I had trained my mind that failing could surprisingly benefit my progression. Before then, I was a lost cause like most people.

Failure would ruin me; it would keep me from wanting to try anything new and outside my comfort zone. It was keeping me from reaching my potential. It was becoming a problem. However, I started to understand this didn't have to be my perception of failure. It doesn't have to be yours either.

4. FOCUS ON POSITIVE SELF-TALK

Many of us tend to create self-limiting beliefs and walls we can't overcome because we tell ourselves we can't do certain things in life. Negative self-talk is a common pattern and habit amongst our society, but you have the ability to put an end to it. You can cut it out of your life.

Your mind, body, and soul is an ecosystem that reacts to the energy surrounding it, including your thoughts. It thrives off positive thinking and positive self-talk. It dwindles from self-shaming, self-sabotaging, and anything negative. Your ecosystem can flourish if you nourish it with positive self-talk, so talk to it positively if you want it to become something bigger than yourself.

5. SURROUND YOURSELF WITH POSITIVE INDIVIDUALS

The power of the people you surround yourself with is one of the most overlooked aspects of positive thinking. The people around you will form the atmosphere you live in. It's highly likely that you'll take on the habits of the people you have strong relationships with and spend the most time with.

So, really, it's simple: Surrounding yourself with positive individuals can turn over a new leaf in your life and materialize a habit of positive thinking.

6. LET GO OF PERFECTION

Perfection is dangerous. Perfection is a recipe for overthinking just about everything in life and never feeling good enough. All it does is program your brain to make you believe that everything in life must be done without mistakes. You must act carefully in your work to avoid hiccups, failures, and setbacks. However, the truth is, you are human and mistakes are inevitable. Imperfection is normal.

Not only is imperfection normal, but it's necessary for us to reach our next stepping stone in our journey. Most of the time when we fall down and make mistakes, we're able to come in contact with things missing from our skill sets, character, and mindset. From making a mistake, we can implement those things into our lives.

Mistakes can be your friend or your enemy. You can let them break you down or guide you to learn crucial things for your growth. But perfection will beat you in the end—it will teach you that you're never good enough because there will always be something to fix.

We live in a time where positive thinking is being pushed heavily. Sometimes, I agree that it can be a little much and overwhelming. However, in small doses, it's incredibly beneficial and important. It's easy to push it off to the side and not make it a life priority. If you fall into the category of people who say, "I'll start tomorrow," it's time you start today—now.

Negative thoughts close your brain off from a lot of the outside world and focus on negative emotions such as fear, anger, and stress. These negative emotions prevent your brain from seeing any other options and choices that surround you. They keep you from reaching your fullest potential. Now, we don't want that, do we?

Positive thoughts do the exact opposite of that. They hone in on positive emotions like joy, contentment, love, and self-worth. These positive emotions allow your brain to see your world from a refreshing perspective that encourages new opportunities. They allow you to step into your power and make unlocking the best version of yourself an achievable reality.

If there's anything you leave with after reading this section, remember this: Positive thoughts will propel you forward and negative thoughts have an equal and opposite force that will set you back. Be intentional with your thoughts; you're the architect of your world.

"
MINDSET MATTERS.

#20
CULTIVATE VALUABLE RELATIONSHIPS

If you're at all familiar with Tim Ferriss, who is an entrepreneur, podcaster, and author of several New York Times Best Sellers like *The 4-Hour Workweek*, then you may know that he ends every episode of The Tim Ferriss Show with a very specific question: "If you could have one billboard anywhere and it could say anything, what would be on it?"

First off, great question. Secondly, that question is difficult for me because there are many different phrases I'd want to put up. A lot of different themes come to mind—success, acceptance, confidence, positivity, and relationships. Truthfully, if I could, I would create several billboards—one for each of those themes. However, that's not in the rules of the game, and I don't feel like bending them right now.

When I sit down and genuinely think about this, something I give high value to is the power of connection and the importance of cultivating honest and genuine relationships. Growing up, my father taught me that it's the people you know who will take you to the next level. He always said, "Life's just one big referral." In other words, your network is your net worth.

What that really means is a large part of growing personally and professionally comes from connecting with likeminded individuals who have aspirations similar to or bigger than yours. These types of relationships will help you connect with other people who are further along in their journey than you are. Not to mention, cultivating genuine connections means other people will have more than a good word to say about you—it's the perfect referral pitch.

So, if I could have one billboard anywhere and it could say anything, it would say: "Cultivate valuable relationships."

Relationships, or social networks, support happiness, success, growth, learning, and pushing the envelope when it comes to becoming the best version of yourself. If you can build a network of people who motivate you to be happy, successful, experience growth, continue to learn, and work on being the best person you can be, then you've pretty much hit a gold mine. I mean, I know I aspire to experience all of those things consistently through my own community, and I hope you do too.

I first began to realize the importance of human connection when I was on my comfort zone hiatus and jumping from country to country while solo backpacking. Being completely isolated from my typical social network of friends, I felt lonely and was missing an important piece of my everyday life.

I knew the only way out of this minor (and temporary) slump was to focus on the power of connection and develop a new network for my current reality. With this mindset, I began to view each individual as an opportunity to connect and broaden my network—increase my overall net worth. I approached them with kindness and listened to them intently to show I cared about what they had to say. This was only the beginning of cultivating valuable relationships.

The relationships I built with individuals from other countries around the world are some of the strongest bonds I've experienced aside from those within my network in the United States. They exist on a much deeper level than anything I've ever experienced before, and I consider them some of my most prized relationships.

These valuable and intentional relationships are the types you can pick up like you saw each other yesterday and have conversations that explore the most genuine parts of life. They continue to change my life and encourage me to cultivate similar relationships with people whom I cross paths with every day. Not only that, but they motivate me to pass along my understanding of the power of human connection to people like you.

You may be thinking, *What did you do after the initial interaction? How did you grow that relationship over time into something incredibly valuable?* Very valid question. There were a few things I held close to me in this process that gave me the opportunity to build relationships that still exist in this very moment, thousands of miles away. Here are five ways you can cultivate valuable, powerful, and intentional relationships:

1. GIVE WITHOUT EXPECTING ANYTHING IN RETURN

The expectation of receiving can be dangerous to the health of a relationship. If you give expecting something in return and don't receive anything, it's likely this will create resentment toward another individual. Resentment is the quickest route toward destroying any chances of building a valuable relationship.

Now, let's take a different approach. Although we know you must give to receive, it's important that we give without expecting anything in return. Sounds contradicting, but let's dive in a bit more. Having high expectations is a great way to set yourself up for failure. We all know when expectations are not met, it's easy to feel let down. So drop your expectations and give from the heart; give because you want the receiving end to feel special.

You see, this is where it gets exciting and where I believe you always get something in return, even if you don't expect it or necessarily need it. If we move our focus away from receiving material goods in return, we will more than likely always receive gratitude from the other individual. This is more than enough. Receiving gratitude is one of the most refreshing gifts you could earn.

So next time you're gifting something, do it because you want to lift up the spirits of someone else, and you may just receive the same feeling, too.

2. SHOW OTHERS THAT YOU CARE

I think it's safe to say feeling cared for goes a very long way. Who doesn't like to be looked after? Who doesn't like to have friends that give you the attention you deserve? I know I do, and I hope you do too because it makes you feel incredibly loved.

Remember how much you enjoy this feeling when interacting in your own relationships—friends, family, and significant others. Know they want to feel cared for too. Most people will recognize their relationships that offer this kind of support.

Offering this in a relationship will present a ton of value to both you and the other individual. It demonstrates that you think about someone, their feelings, and what they may need to feel safe in their own life. Don't take this with a grain of salt. The care you give to another individual is a trophy quality in cultivating powerful and valuable relationships.

3. FIND COMMONALITIES AND DETERMINE HOW YOU CAN USE THEM TO GROW WITH AN INDIVIDUAL

A big part of relationships is growing individually but also growing together—as a team. For me, I focus a lot on the teammate aspect of a relationship, whether that's with my significant other, friends, or family.

The best way to create that teammate feeling is to work on discovering the things two people have in common—you and another person. This could be hobbies, books, music, food, exercise, or art. It can be anything you find in common that you can use to leverage growth together.

Whatever it is you find in common, think of it as the center of your relationship—the thing that you both revolve around. Consider this the relationship's north star and let it guide you into cultivating something incredible. Let this give the relationships a sense of purpose, and you'll soon see it flourish. Remember, this is a team effort. Grow collectively and use your commonalities as the compass to building an intentional relationship.

4. CONNECT WITH PEOPLE EVEN IF YOU BELIEVE YOU WON'T GET SOMETHING FROM IT

I think a lot of the time people only want to connect with someone if they will get something in return. This relates perfectly to giving without expecting something in return. Too many times, people think they should get something in return when they give someone else their time. But this is the wrong approach to building intentional relationships. You're already setting your expectations too high and increasing the probability to be let down. Instead, do the opposite and something magical might happen.

Many times when we have lower expectations, there's a plethora of unexpected experiences that bring us a lot of happiness and fulfillment. What's better than going into a situation and getting something extraordinary in return? Not sure, but from purposely lowering my expectations, I've had this happen on several occasions. Dozens of the strong and valuable relationships I have with people now developed from a single conversation that I wasn't expecting to get anything from.

But really, there are two reasons I think it's beneficial to connect with people even if you believe you won't get something from it: 1) it may open the door to an entirely new and unexpected relationship that would have never come into your reality if you didn't connect, and 2) although you may not get something from it, there's a very real possibility the other individual could receive something they need—something that can change their life.

So when you're thinking of the reasons you shouldn't connect with someone, stop and tell yourself those excuses are bullshit. It's not going to hurt you, so might as well just offer your time.

5. BE MINDFUL AND LOOK OUT FOR OPPORTUNITIES NOT ONLY FOR YOURSELF, BUT FOR OTHERS, TOO

One of the best feelings in a relationship is when someone tells you they heard about an opportunity and immediately thought about you. Intentional and valuable relationships involve looking out for one another. And, no, I don't just mean looking after one's safety, I also mean thinking about their career and what opportunities they're seeking.

If you want to form one of the most genuine and beneficial relationships with another individual, be mindful of them even when they're not around. Actually, that's the most crucial time to be mindful of them. That's an indicator that you truly care and believe in the strength of a relationship. People recognize these types of actions and they never go unnoticed.

So, although it's important to be seeking new opportunities for yourself, seek for others too if you want to build a valuable relationship. Not only will this open doors for others (the people you're building a relationship with), but it will also open doors for your character. This is a quality that's hard to come by but incredible when discovered. People will notice your mindfulness and be inspired to practice it too.

Intentional living comes from being conscious of your actions and mindful of how you approach different aspects of life. With the five action items listed above, you can begin to focus on building both current and new relationships. Whether you're struggling to find your path or looking to elevate your current life, relationships are an important building block to progress.

The goal should be to surround yourself with people who support your journey and vice versa. Find people who understand your highest desires and people who you understand, too. The relationship must be mutual for it to be beneficial. If not, then one person will slowly begin to feel unwanted, unappreciated, and as if the other isn't contributing to the greater good of the relationship.

Remember, your network is your net worth, so it's important to fill it with individuals who will increase your intangible wealth or, what I like to call, your character. Find people who vibrate on the same wavelength and are on a mission for more. Find people who understand you, just as well as you understand them. And when you find those people, give without expecting anything in return, show them you care, grow together, and always be mindful of them. That's the recipe to relationships that can't be broken.

So, yes, if I could have one billboard anywhere and it could say anything, it would say "Cultivate valuable relationships." Everyone deserves to learn the power of human connection. I was lucky enough to learn this at a very young age from my father, and it's helped me immensely with my professional and personal growth. I can confidently say I'm not sure where I would be without the people I've met and continue to grow relationships with. They elevate my life, and I hope I do the same for them.

View every new relationship as an opportunity to increase your net worth. At the end of the day, the people you know can take you to unimaginable places. Life's just one big referral.

99

LIFE'S ONE BIG REFERRAL.

#21
CHOOSE YOUR ATMOSPHERE

If we want to achieve a certain life or implement specific changes, we must create that world for ourselves. We can't expect our reality to shift into something we desire by sitting around and being passive. We must be active in developing an atmosphere that will promote exactly what we want—success, happiness, positive change, passion, purpose, growth, you name it. Creating your personal atmosphere starts with the choices you make that dictate what you do on a daily basis.

Everything in life revolves around choices. We all have the freedom to choose, but not everyone has that understanding. You control your day, and it's in your power to decide how you'll act, carry yourself, and react to the different situations you encounter. However, often times, we wish someone else could make life choices for us, but that's not practical.

When we choose not to choose, we surrender one of our greatest gifts—the freedom of choice. You give up the power to choose who you want to be and how you want to live. When you let that happen you might as well hang up the cleats, because your life is no longer yours.

We must take on the responsibility of choosing because it's in our power to create the atmosphere we live in—an intentional lifestyle. So, yes, we are looking at two things here: intentional choices and an intentional lifestyle. They go hand-in-hand because you can't create an intentional lifestyle without focusing on intentional choices. Kapeesh?

We are going to reverse engineer this topic and first deconstruct the importance of an intentional lifestyle. That seems to be a solid approach to demonstrate why you would want to practice your freedom to choose. Let's talk about how powerful and important your lifestyle is before teaching you how to get there. Again, reverse engineering—starting from the end and working our way back to the lesson on how to make intentional choices to invent your desired lifestyle.

So, what's lifestyle? According to Merriam-Webster, lifestyle is the "typical way of life of an individual, group, or culture." Bland, boring, lame. Let's spice that up a bit. Lifestyle is the combination of your behaviors, interests, and opinions that make up an atmosphere that promotes your most desired way of living. In the simplest terms, lifestyle is the way you live, why you live, and the manner in which you carry yourself.

Your lifestyle can help define not only your path but also the integrity of your journey down your path. It can set the tone of your existence, and it's a crucial influencer when it comes to inventing the life you want. Lifestyle changes are what you need to get to your next stepping stone. Without these changes, your life will remain the same. And if you're reading this book, I can guess there's at least one thing in your life you wish was different.

Choosing the atmosphere and specific lifestyle you want will help you become who you want to be. By choosing these things you give yourself permission to be the very best version of yourself.

If you want to be a writer, give yourself permission to think like a writer. If you want to be a motivational speaker, give yourself permission to think like a motivational speaker. If you want to become the best version of yourself, then give yourself permission to think like the absolute best version of yourself. The process doesn't need to be complicated. Just grant yourself the permission to be who you want to be.

But, with that permission, you must also implement a lifestyle that supports the thing you want to do. When I was becoming a writer and taking that first step toward achieving the goal, I had to teach myself to think like a writer. With no writing background, it was tough but not impossible. However, I knew that to make it a reality, I needed to choose and create an atmosphere that supported the dream. I needed to make some serious changes to develop an intentional lifestyle.

I started with the obvious: writing more often to become a writer—doing the verb to be the noun. But besides that, there are several other aspects that can promote a lifestyle that supports becoming a writer. Things that came to mind immediately were a clear mind, a healthy body, productivity, reducing self-pressure and stress, and eating nutrient-rich foods.

You're probably wondering how these things relate to developing a writer-like lifestyle. I'm happy to tell you they all helped me get to where I wanted to be. All these things helped me create an atmosphere—an intentional lifestyle—that allowed me to evolve into my best version.

The good thing about this story is that the five lifestyle changes below can apply to anyone and any situation. These changes promote a higher state of living and, by incorporating them into my own life, I experienced how beneficial they can be when it comes to taking a stand to create an intentional lifestyle:

1. USE WEEKENDS TO YOUR ADVANTAGE (AS MUCH AS POSSIBLE)

I would say the masses typically work rather demanding hours throughout the week, taking up much of their free time. Although pretty much unavoidable, there are ways to win yourself some free time if you stay disciplined.

If you work long hours throughout the week, weekends are a glimpse of freedom. No one looking over your shoulder, no one asking you to clock in, no one asking for your time, none of that. I like to look at the weekends as a vacation—a two day vacation every five days. How great is that?

Yet, too often, weekend time is used inefficiently. This is especially true for those who want to work on themselves and improve or grow on their path of unlocking their fullest potential. Although I view weekends as a vacation, it's mostly a vacation from my full-time job. When I see two full days (Saturday and Sunday) with nothing on the agenda, it's like I'm getting a birthday cake minus the birthday.

However, there are also people who don't work a normal 9-to-5 job, and you may fall into that category. You may actually not have a free 48 hours on the weekends, whether you're working a freelance gig, parenting children, or doing anything else that takes up your Saturdays and Sundays. But you can still use time blocking and dedicate one, two, or three hours of the weekend to yourself. In my mind, any amount of time you can use to your advantage is a win.

If you want to become the best version of yourself, then you should carve out a few hours each day to work on yourself or your craft. Sure, it may feel like a lot at first, but when the day is over, I guarantee you won't regret the work completed. It's not supposed to be easy, but if you really want it, you'll find the discipline and choose to take advantage of your weekends.

2. WALKS ARE COOL, ASK SNOOP DOGG

A friend once said they didn't go for walks. They believed walks were a complete waste of time. I also once heard a story about screenwriter and producer Evan Goldberg (Seth Rogen's better half) and Snoop Dogg (yes, Snoop D.O. Double G.) who were in a room together when Snoop Dogg asked Goldberg if he went on walks. Goldberg quickly answered, "No." And that's when it all happened.

Snoop Dogg looked at him with the most disappointed expression, as if his own son had just let him down. Goldberg said Snoop Dogg's disappointment haunts him to this day. Since that conversation, he takes multiple walks every day and admits it has completely changed his life.

First off, yes that's a completely true story. Secondly, walks are a great way to clear your mind, step away from something stressful, and an easy way to implement breaks in your day. This small action can help you immensely, and you can use them to reset your mind or even to ponder your deepest thoughts on the next best step to take in your journey. So yes, take walks, and if you think they're worthless, just remember Snoop Dogg's disappointment.

3. FOCUS ON ORGANIZING YOUR OWN LIFE

It's safe to say a lot of us don't have our shit together; many areas of life are messy and unorganized. Having a bearing on what's going on in your life is vital when you want to take a leap for a bigger challenge. When I wanted to take on more, I knew I needed to organize my own life. I discovered that I needed to optimize my day and iron out my misused time. I spent lots of time engulfed in my phone or simply finding excuses to push off what I needed to do.

Productivity is important whether you want to prove your worth for another promotion at work or find more time to spend with your family. You need to find ways to allocate your time intentionally to be able to put your energy toward important aspects of life that will take you to the next level.

To remedy my misuse of time, I began to time block my days. This means I create time slots to do specific tasks—work- and life-related. Time blocking lets me use every minute of my day intentionally and achieve the absolute most productivity.

Organizing your own life can be key to making time to focus on the things that will allow you to unlock your full potential. From overcoming my own unorganized day, I guarantee the three or four hours you spend on your phone every day or the excuses you make up to push valuable tasks off until later isn't worth it. All you're doing is running away from what could be the open door into an entirely different life—the one you've been seeking. Hold yourself accountable for how you use your time. Become the master of your day.

4. EATING REGIMEN

Food is medicine, and what you put in your body will alter your mood, emotions, mental clarity, and overall well-being. Now, I'm not a medical doctor, dietitian, or nutritionist, so I have no certifications or licenses that give me the credibility to inform you how to eat. But I do feel comfortable and okay with shining light on the "why" of eating in a way that improves your clarity and overall health.

Typically, when we're on the path to finding our purpose, passion, or where we belong, it takes a lot of energy and discipline. It's important to choose an eating lifestyle that promotes mental clarity and extended energy.

The things we put in our bodies—food, liquids, and anything of that sort—play a key role in shaping the way we're able to manage how we move through our days. The thing is everyone's eating lifestyle or eating regimen will vary because no single body is the same. We all crave different things at different times for different reasons. It's a puzzle we must all solve on our own, but finding that solution can put us in the right headspace we need to keep us motivated and energized to becoming the best version of ourselves. You must take care of what's on the inside first before you approach external forces in your life. Your body is a temple.

5. WORK-LIFE INTEGRATION

When most people talk about work and life, it's about the classic "work-life balance." Although this is right, and is an excellent approach for separating the two, I think there are times when you can integrate them to help you grow.

When I think of my job and my life, I focus on work-life integration. How can I bring the two together in a way that they support each other? What can I take from work that can help improve my life? What can I take from my life that can help improve my work? All questions I believe we should always be asking. This helps keep us moving forward in both areas.

The better approach to this philosophy is the comparison between professional growth and personal growth, which will help demonstrate how work-life integration can be simple.

For me, if I become the best version of myself in my personal life, I'll be able to show up as a better person in the workplace, and therefore experience professional growth more easily. In contrast to that, if I choose to be a shitty person outside of work, then I sure as hell won't give a damn about my professional growth when I walk through those office doors.

Personal growth can be derived from your profession if you focus on implementing applicable things you learn at work into your personal life. This can be things like how to manage people, solve complex problems, and command respect without being a jerk. All we need to do for that to happen? Set an intention to choose to develop a healthy and beneficial work-life integration.

So great, now you know the importance of lifestyle changes and been introduced to some of the ones I've found most beneficial through self-experimentation. Remember, though, it's important to find what lifestyle works for you and to choose the changes that will push you further in your personal journey. These choices must be intentional, as the lifestyle changes will serve a high purpose when it comes to opening the door to your fullest potential.

There's also a very simple three-step process I follow in most of my decision making. It helps me evaluate what's at stake and yields the most potential for making intentional choices.

Intentional choices and an intentional lifestyle should be methodical. Assessing the outcome—both negative and positive—is important to any sort of decision making, whether the decision be large or small. Always approach every choice with equal integrity, as your decisions will shape the reality that exists around you. A simple process like this can help you make intentional choices:

1. PREPARE TO CHOOSE AND REMEMBER THE "WHY"

One of the most important things, not only in making choices, but in life overall, is remembering the "why" in different situations. The "why" is what reminds you of the purpose and serves as a nudge to stay on track. It can keep you in close understanding with the direction you're headed or the direction you want to work toward going. Let it be your north star as you prepare to make an intentional choice.

Ask yourself: Why am I taking a step to make this intentional choice?

2. EVALUATE THE OUTCOME, BENEFITS, AND REPERCUSSIONS

The reality is that not everything will have a beneficial outcome. Unfortunately, sometimes life throws us curve balls and messes up all of our plans. Now, I'm not saying the chances of a negative outcome are more likely than the chances of a positive outcome. I'm saying both are a possibility.

With that being said, when you're making a choice, it's a good step to evaluate all outcomes of that choice—benefits and repercussions. Understanding the outcome of a choice and making a mindful decision can help increase the chances of implementing changes in your life that will have a net benefit to your personal growth.

3. FOLLOW THROUGH WITH YOUR CHOICE

Finally, if you've recognized your choice will provide a net benefit to your growth, follow through. The last thing you want is to be someone who says they're going to do something and never does. Cultivate the quality of executing the important things in life, as they can play a key role in finding your path, purpose, and the best version of yourself.

While some may think this is just a way to overthink your choices, it's not. Using a method to choose changes in your life will help yield a higher chance of those choices being beneficial to your journey. While we're on the path to becoming the best versions of ourselves, it's important to do everything we can in our power to choose things that will catapult us forward—get us to the next stepping stone.

This three-step method can transfer to any type of decision making, not just ones that revolve around intentional lifestyle changes. It can be used in your work environment, relationships, to help you decide the best way to use your time on a daily basis, to help refine and elevate your craft, you name it.

Although sometimes we think we can't choose because some limits in life are imposed based on our values, beliefs, and the commitments we've made, there's always a possibility. Choices don't always need to result in a physical or tangible result. Some decisions we make in life will remain internal forever.

Even if you are experiencing limitations of your choices, you still have the freedom to choose how you'll react to something and how it will impact you mentally and emotionally. Remember, there's an entire world and ecosystem that lives within us, and we must do our best to protect it from the external forces that may want to impede its well-being.

>

YOUR CHOICES EMPOWER YOU.

#22
BUILD YOUR SYSTEM

It takes 21 days to form a habit. It takes 30 days to form a habit. It takes 60 days to form a habit. It takes...yeah we get it. We've heard it all. Forget the number of days it takes to form a habit. You know what it takes? It takes heart, it takes discipline, it takes passion. It takes a deep desire to want to make a change. Sure it takes time, but more importantly, it takes every ounce of you.

Stop relying on the number of days it's going to take to form a habit and focus on the amount of energy you need to spend to get there. It's tough, but habits are the building blocks of achieving something. They're the system we all must build to reach our goals.

Let's set this straight. Unfortunately, the chance of forming bad habits is just as likely as forming good habits. However, bad habits typically form from lack of effort, repeated negative behavioral patterns, and an unwillingness to change for the better. All of which are completely in your control. You have the ability to choose between forming good or bad habits solely through your actions. The ball is in your court, and it's waiting for you to make your next move.

Sure, forming good, intentional habits can be difficult. It would be completely wrong for me to say otherwise, so let's accept that now. However, difficult does not mean impossible. Difficult means there will be several hurdles to leap over with a reward waiting near the end. To me, something challenging is something worth chasing. It's bound to bring you fulfillment upon completion. And, for something like good habits, we need to drop the fear of the challenge because they play such an important role in our journey toward completing our goals.

Before we even approach goals, we must face our habits. Without positive behavioral patterns, the probability of completing something challenging is second to none. It's almost imperative to build a system first before setting our goals. If goals are set without a foundation of good habits, you're just setting yourself up to come up short. You are not giving yourself the necessary resources you'll need to complete your goal. So, let's start from ground zero—forming good, intentional habits.

Wanting to form a good habit can derive from two different situations: 1) you've realized the behavioral patterns in your everyday life are not supporting your journey and 2) you want to build a system that's going to allow you to become the best version of yourself—and achieve your goals. Luckily, the processes for both of these reasons are more or less identical. And it starts now. Why? Because you deserve this shit.

Most of us have an understanding (taught by our lovely society) that there's this golden window of time in which a good habit forms. However, that doesn't sit with me well—it never really has. Because at the base of it all, forming new, intentional habits is the process of learning something new. We're all uniquely different, which means processes in each of our lives will also vary. Our brains work differently, our bodies respond differently, and, most importantly, some people climb learning curves faster than others (and that's okay).

So, let's drop the "it takes 21 days, 30 days, 60 days to form a habit." Let's draw our attention away from the timeline because deadlines (especially on things that don't need them) create unnecessary and unneeded pressure on a task that should be completed at a pace that yields the most valuable results. Instead, let's focus on the amount of effort we're going to put forth during our habit building, and surrender to the process of building a system that will support your biggest goals—your dreams.

When we are learning something as important as the habits that will carry us further on our path, it's best to approach it with a method. This is something I call *strategic habit forming*.

Strategic habit forming is the process of developing a method of learning that resonates with your unique way of being and helps elevate your future system. It involves understanding how you work best in situations that encompass a great deal of new things. If we approach things in life that are challenging without a method or strategy to complete it, we create room to do the exact opposite—not succeed.

However, strategic habit forming doesn't have to be a shot in the dark. You don't have to guess how to approach it and how to make it work. Similar to making intentional choices, there's a pattern of stages that can help you fully grasp this theory. For me, whether I'm forming new habits, working on positive thinking, or making impactful decisions, defined actionable steps help me understand exactly what I need to do for me to succeed.

Actionable steps are like the street signs we see on our everyday roads that direct us in the right direction. Without them, we'd be a lost puppy guessing our next move. But with them, it's an entirely different story. We can feel more confident with each step we take because the signs—actionable steps—give us the energy to progress confidently.

Luckily, strategic habit forming consists of just that—four actionable steps that can take a new behavioral pattern and turn it into second nature. Through these four steps, you'll be able to implement new habits into your life that can be beneficial to discovering your own journey and becoming the best version of yourself:

1. ASKING THE RIGHT QUESTIONS

Anytime we introduce something new into our lives, we must first familiarize ourselves with it and how it may impact other areas. The same goes for intentional, new habits. We need to assess the habit we want to incorporate and ask the right questions. This will not only help give an early indication of the benefits it may add to our lives, but also the old habits we will need to drop. Often, forming new habits is a solution to replace old behavior patterns that don't serve you.

So before you even think of starting on the path to forming the new habit, ask yourself some questions to understand what you may be getting yourself into. How will this impact my relationships? What old habits will I need to escape? What must I start doing every day that I don't do already? How will this new habit serve my life? Am I willing to devote the dedication and discipline involved in forming this new habit?

These questions will help you grasp what it will actually take to form a new habit, and it will bring to the surface any repercussions or benefits.

2. INCORPORATING THE HABIT IN YOUR LIFE

The next step is the leap of faith step—incorporating the habit into your life. Typically difficult at first, it's important to give yourself the proper time to let it flourish. There's no reason to set a deadline. This is something that you should handle with care to reap the most benefits. Slowly ease the new habit into your everyday life. It will feel uncomfortable at first and, if you're like me, you'll want to give up immediately. But don't.

Don't give up because it will be worth it. Don't give up because you are a strong, passionate, and driven individual that craves positive change. Don't give up because you are taking strides that will lead you further down your own journey. Don't give up because these new, intentional habits will create opportunity for personal growth. Don't give up because you are more capable than you believe. Don't give up because you are finally standing up to your life and demanding purpose. Don't give up because you *can* do it. Don't give up because you deserve this shit.

3. UNDERSTANDING HOW YOUR HABIT WILL SERVE YOU

With time, your new habit is going to start to feel familiar. You'll start to experience the ease of it existing in your life. Now, just because things are starting to become comfortable doesn't mean you should sit back and relax. You're not on habit vacation quite yet.

When you start to see a habit form in your life become, well for lack of a better word, habitual—a behavioral pattern—it's time to push forward more. At this moment, you're almost to a point where you can let off the gas pedal and let the new habit do its work. But not yet.

Once your new habit becomes more intertwined with your life, it's time to step back and evaluate your vision of how it will serve you moving forward. Think of it this way: each habit is its own project and you should look at how it will perform over the days, months, or years, and plan how it will serve your life.

What do you need to do to maintain the habit? How will the new habit create more space for other positive changes? How will this habit elevate your journey? These are just a few questions to ask yourself in this process.

This will allow you to understand its importance and realize how this habit can create positive change in your life. When we come in contact with the impact something can have on our life, we tend to hold it to a higher importance—it becomes a *real* priority. That's exactly what we want to do with new habits. You want to get to a point where the habit lives within you—a new way of living.

4. AUTO PILOT

Great, now you've got the new habit up and running. It's feeling more comfortable and you're not spending as much energy trying to implement it into your life. It's becoming less of a task and more of a piece of your character. That's exactly where you want to be.

Forming new habits shouldn't be a process that lasts forever. Your main goal should be to reach a point of auto pilot so you can start the process over with another new, intentional habit. Because, if you're in any way like me, then you know there are an infinite amount of habits you can work into your life.

There's a point in time where your habit goes in auto pilot mode—it becomes second nature. Once you cross this point of forming a new habit, the behavior can be done more or less without thinking. This allows you to take your mind off your repetition and practice because the habit has reached its full evolution. It's now a part of your life—a new habit has been formed.

Although those four steps of strategic habit forming are usually my bread and butter for implementing something new into my life, there's one secret ingredient to the recipe: repetition. Without it, you might as well consider the effort in trying to develop a new habit a loss because repetition is necessary to form any new, intentional habits.

Too many of us want to be perfect. We don't want to fail, especially at something we know will benefit our journey. But remember this: Let go of perfection. Perfection isn't something to chase since it's too often a recipe for coming up short and believing we are not good enough.

Same goes for forming new habits, let go of perfection. Perfection isn't an ingredient of the recipe. If we approach the goal of forming a new habit with the idea that we're going to achieve perfection, we are already starting off on the wrong foot. Cultivating the idea of perfection creates a system that's far too likely to fail. We need to build a system that gives us the highest potential to achieve our biggest goals.

The whole idea around forming new, intentional habits is to create behavioral patterns that will aid you along your path to becoming the best version of yourself. These behavioral patterns will shape the system that supports your goals and your dreams. Without your system, you can still create goals, but the road to reach those goals is windy and can be easily broken.

To successfully form new habits—build your system—focus on practice, not perfection. You need to practice these new habits over and over again until they become a natural part of your life—second nature. Throughout your practice, I'm sure you'll experience some failure, which is normal. But continue to practice because you'll begin to see that the secret ingredient to forming any new habit is repetition and not perfection.

> **FOCUS ON REPETITION NOT PERFECTION.**

#23
YOUR LIFE WILL BE AS BIG AS YOUR ASPIRATIONS

The trajectory of your path and life revolves around the height at which you aim to reach. Aim low and you'll only achieve things that are about par with everyone else. Aim high and the potential of experiencing a miracle is second to none. And when you aim high, expect a miracle; believe that you deserve to experience something a lot of us would only recognize in a dream.

I think it's too common in life for us to aim with caution; we are scared that chasing a dream too big will result in failure that we can't recuperate from. That's a thought pattern we need to overcome to achieve our ultimate success in any of our endeavors.

The goals you aim to achieve in life create the atmosphere around your journey. They create the world you live in. Your goals set the tone of your quest and will be an indicator of the magnitude of your potential achievements.

Once we've built a system that can support our deepest desires, it's time to dream big. It's time to focus on creating the goals that will allow us to unlock our greatest potential and become the best versions of ourselves. You have the choice to reach for the stars or aim cautiously. But, do know this: Your life will only be as big as your aspirations.

We need to set our goals intentionally, which means creating action steps that make the end goal attainable and real. It's common for people to set lofty goals and figure with time they will magically get there, but soon enough they realize they've fallen off track.

You may have experienced something similar with New Year's resolutions. I know I have. For example, every time I set New Year's resolutions, they seem to slowly disintegrate month after month and then vanish into thin air before I can complete or achieve them. Why? Because like most people, my resolutions didn't involve the most crucial component to achieving the goal: action steps.

After years of failed resolutions, I did away with them and turned to goal setting. Goal setting is a much more attainable approach to achieve one, or many, of your aspirations. While there are several types of goals, such as time-based goals and SMART goals (Specific, Measurable, Achievable, Relevant, and Time-bound), there was one goal setting formula I found worked tremendously in my favor. Finally, here was something to replace my half-assed New Year's resolutions. This method involves identifying a goal, defining the milestone, and creating actionable steps that will make your goal and milestone attainable.

Too often people set goals with an undefined path, which leads them in no true direction. What I've learned in my own journey of goal setting is the importance of working backwards from your milestone. This will help create the steps needed to achieve your goal and feel accomplished. What this means is if you want to start at point A and end up at point B, then in your goal setting exercise you actually need to start with point B and work your way back toward point A. Confused? Worried? Don't be.

To help, review the two examples below that illustrate a specific goal, a defined milestone, and the action steps that are necessary to get you from point A to point B:

EXAMPLE 1

Goal: Save more money
Milestone: Save $10,000 in one year
Step 1: Calculate how much money you need to save per month (roughly $833/month).
Step 2: Find ways to increase your income, reduce expenses, and minimize debt to meet this amount monthly.
Step 3: Create a financial plan and budget that supports your monthly savings goal.
Step 4: Save roughly $833 per month to reach your milestone—save $10,000 in one year.

EXAMPLE 2

Goal: Grow your email subscriber list

Milestone: Grow your email subscriber list of 100 people by 500% in one year

Step 1: Calculate how many new subscribers you need per month (500 subscribers in 12 months or roughly 42 subscribers per month to reach 600 subscribers).

Step 2: Create and find ways to increase your subscriber list through email marketing tools and email capture popups.

Step 3: Purchase any email marketing tools, such as OptinMonster, to help capture readers' emails.

Step 4: Grow email list by publishing one high-quality article per week to hit your milestone—500 new email subscribers in one year—and maintain current subscribers by sending out one valuable newsletter per week.

Goals are not cookie cutter. The goals you set must not only resonate with you, but you must also understand that each step requires different amounts of energy and focus. Goals, milestones, and their steps are not one-size-fits-all. However, all goals should involve the necessary steps you need to take to achieve your aspirations.

Now, your goals may shift as you get older and that's okay. The goals you set at age 20 are going to be completely different than the goals you set at age 30 and 40. Life is short, and it moves quickly. What you wanted yesterday may not be what you want tomorrow. But that's normal. Our surroundings—people, jobs, inspirations—tend to play a role in the things we're able to envision for our lives. Embrace the potential shift of your goals. Reassess them often to maintain a clear understanding of what direction you're heading.

Along with your goals transforming with the trajectory of your life, they should also evolve as we reach them. This promotes continuous progression. If you reach your goal but don't evolve it into something bigger, all you do is close a door on more opportunity. You tell yourself there's nothing more you can achieve—you create a ceiling.

As we achieve and reach our goals, it's important to keep them going and build on top of them. For example, in example one the goal was to save $10,000 in one year. Once you save $10,000, if you want to push yourself forward more, begin to think of the next evolution of this goal—saving $15,000, $20,000, or $25,000.

In example two, the goal was to grow your email subscriber list by 500%. When you achieve that goal, it's important to set a new goal to grow it by a new amount. This will help you push further and achieve something above your original aspiration.

A question that I ask often and find helpful in these types of situations is, "What's next?" What else can come from this goal? How can I evolve my original goal to create more room for progression and achievement? Where do I want to be two, five, or 10 years from now?

These types of questions can help you to tap into more opportunities that you didn't know existed. You'll be able to realize that achieving the initial goal doesn't mean you've reached the end of the journey. While it's important to celebrate your victories and be proud of what you've accomplished, it's equally important to keep your mind challenged with a fresh new goal at hand.

As humans we crave incremental progress, and goals allow us to quench that appetite for progress. Setting intentional goals can help create a natural motivator in your life. Your visions, dreams, and aspirations will shape the reality of the world you live in and open you up to manifestation. So don't aim low, and don't aim cautiously. Write that book. Make that movie. Start that podcast. Play music until you're a headliner. Do what it is in your mind that makes you feel like you're chasing your biggest dream.

Dream up your best life scenario. You've got one real chance to do it, and your time is now. The people you idolize and aspire to be like—celebrities and public figures—are just like you. We're all human, but those individuals have worked their ass off and continued to dream as big as possible. Use them as proof that you can do the same. At one point in their life they debated whether or not to go after their wildest dreams. My guess is they chose to say "I can" and never said "I can't."

So next time you're contemplating whether to chase a dream or not, ask yourself this: "Will my future self regret not doing this?" And if your answer is "yes," then go for it.

You're just one "I can" away from a miracle.

> **YOUR GOALS SET THE TONE OF YOUR QUEST.**

#24
INTENTIONAL LIVING: WHAT YOU CAN DO WITH THESE LESSONS

Intentional living truthfully derives from your mindset and the conscious energy you put forth into your decisions. In this last section, we discussed several lessons that show you where in your life you can become more intentional. Intentional living is truly the final puzzle piece and last pillar of your self-discovery. It was the last quality I discovered on my own journey, and I wanted to make it the last for you, too.

Although there's a possibility that not all of these lessons resonate with you, I dare say there's at least one from this section that can create a positive change in your life today. It's time to act on those lessons—whether that's one or several—and implement this new way of living. Trust me. It's going to feel damn good.

In this chapter, I created different action items to help you jumpstart your journey of intentional living and further your own self-discovery. These are aspects I've included in my own life, and I've experienced incredible changes from these steps. They're not impossible. However, that doesn't mean they won't be challenging at first. Be okay with the challenge. Be okay with slow results. Over time, you'll see this new way of living leads to something amazing—an intentional life that benefits you and others. These six action items will help you cultivate intention into your life moving forward:

1. **Create a morning routine:** The easiest way to be in the driver seat of your day is to create a morning practice that gives you the keys. Morning routines can help improve your attitude, performance, and overall energy. So why would you not have one? Be sure to create a morning routine that works for your goals and schedule. But when you're doing so, there are a few things to keep in mind:

   1) Set barriers and boundaries
   2) Turn off your phone
   3) Incorporate one ritual-like action into your morning routine, such as brewing coffee, making tea, or meditation
   4) Be consistent

   These four items allowed me to create the most optimal and beneficial morning routine, and I believe they can do the same for you, too. (Chapter 18)

2. **Practice positive thinking:** Your thoughts are energy. They cause change both internally and externally—your mind and your actions. Your mindset truly matters, and it can be a powerful aspect to unlocking the maximum version of your character. To incorporate positive thinking into your life, use these steps to your advantage:

    1. Start the day with positive affirmations
    2. Find gratitude in every situation
    3. Turn failures into lessons
    4. Focus on positive self-talk
    5. Surround yourself with positive individuals
    6. Let go of perfection

    These six items can help you design your life through positive thinking. These are tools and tactics I consistently practice in my own life to make sure I'm doing my absolute best to be in control of my thoughts. You have the power to be in control, too. (Chapter 19)

3. **Build valuable and powerful relationships:** Building valuable relationships and focusing on the power of connection can be a catalyst on your journey. To begin doing this, it's important to give without expecting anything in return. Show others that you care, find commonalities, and determine how you can use those commonalities to grow with an individual. Connect with people even if you believe you won't

get something from it. Be mindful. Look out for opportunities for yourself and others. View every new relationship as a way you can increase your overall net worth. (Chapter 20)
4. **Make decisions that will elevate your lifestyle:** Your choices and decisions can dictate your life's path. If you want to chase a specific life or create change, you must take charge and create that world for yourself through a lifestyle developed by intentional choices. To do so, prepare to choose, remember the "why," evaluate the outcome, benefits, and repercussions, and *always* follow through with your choice. (Chapter 21)
5. **Form habits that support your goals:** We all have our personal goals, whether they relate to your journey of self-discovery or something else. However, to achieve these goals we must form habits—a system—that help us get to where we want to be.

    You can form new, intentional habits by asking the right questions about what habits are missing and what (negative) habits need to go, incorporating the new habit into your life, evaluating its future potential for your life, and letting the habit become second nature. To do this effectively, you must let go of perfection and embrace repetition. (Chapter 22)
6. **Dream big, *really* big:** Anytime you create a vision for yourself, remember that your life will be as big as your aspirations—your dreams. Don't be afraid to dream your wildest dreams, it's these intentions that will take you to your highest potential. You're an

incredible human being, but you need to remember that yourself. I won't always be there to tell you that. Don't sell yourself short, aim high, and chase *exactly* what you want, regardless of how impossible it feels at first. (Chapter 23)

Intentional living was the final pillar of self-discovery I learned along my journey, but it's a never-ending lesson. Every day my intentions seem to reach greater depths and I become aware of how they impact my life. This can be the same for you, too.

With these six action items, you can begin to feel in touch with your intentions and discover ways to be more intentional as you walk your path. It's a refreshing way to live. This lifestyle not only benefits you, but your intentions will also benefit the people in your surrounding community. Bring the power of intention into your life and watch your journey flourish in front of your eyes.

> **LIVING INTENTIONALLY SETS YOU FREE.**

# #25
THIS BOOK IS YOUR NUDGE

Congratulations, you've made it. We've made it. We've made it to the end of the lesson, the end of the class. The honest lessons we've discussed will help you realize the reality of becoming not only you, but the best version of you. It's your turn to take over. It's your turn to implement the actions, lessons, and ideas that resonate with you to create positive change. Although this is the close of the book, it's the beginning of something extraordinary: your journey of unlocking your greatest potential.

The lessons I've shared with you involve personal experiences that have worked tremendously in my favor to help invent my path, purpose, and passion in life. I believe wholeheartedly that with awareness, getting outside your comfort zone, and living intentionally, you can make impactful shifts in your life.

It's your time to shine. You've gathered bits and pieces throughout these pages and some may have resonated more than others. Use the ones you're drawn to as a guide to begin walking your own path. It's been waiting for you to arrive all along.

When you approach your path, look at it with pride. Look at it with excitement, enthusiasm, and the audacity to explore it without fear. Take a stand to make the steps you've always dreamed about taking. This is your path and nobody else's. Treat it like your baby and nurture it often so you can live a life worth living while you still have time left on this planet.

When I think of a life path, I see it visually. It's a long narrow path covered in brown, unpromising dirt. The dirt is somewhat soft near the beginning. Your foot sinks in about an inch or two, which makes for a challenge.

But as you find your way down the path, the dirt becomes more firm. Your foot begins to sink less and less. Soon, you feel supported and begin to question less and less whether your footing is secure. You become more comfortable as you journey down the path.

The path is lined by tall reeds of bamboo with bright green leaves near the top. As you gaze in the distance—as far as you can see—you catch a glimpse of a bright white light. Although you're not sure of its source, you know it's something you must follow.

As you think about this path and its different aspects, challenges, and, most importantly, metaphors, you can draw a relation between this path and the one you're on in your own life.

The soft brown dirt represents the challenges we all face as we start on our journey. Each step we take is difficult in the beginning, but as we gain our confidence we begin to feel grounded and find soil that's more firm. The bamboo illustrates the people in your network, the people who will stand tall for you when you're down. Trust in their guidance, this isn't a solo journey. We're all in this race together.

Finally, you begin to understand that the light in the distance is a sign of where your journey is leading you. It's your future self's greatest life achievement: living your truth and becoming the person you were always meant to be.

It's your time to shine in your own light. It's your time to become the best version of yourself. The doors are there and you can walk through them. You just need to find the courage to turn the door knob and push it open. The only person between you and living the life you've always dreamt of is yourself.

You're responsible for the blueprint of your life. You're the architect of your reality. It's your behavior, your choices, and your decisions that will define the path you walk. It's easy to blame external forces and people for how your life is shaping up. However, at the end of the day, you have the freedom to choose how you react to those forces. That choice is what keeps your life in your hands.

Before we depart and go our opposite ways, there are a few things I want to ask of you:

1. TAKE ACTION

Whether there's one lesson or 100 lessons from this book that resonate with you, get ready to put it or them into play in your life. It's your responsibility to take action on the things you want to change. No one else is going to do it for you. This book was just a class, now it's time for you to put in the work for the positive changes to come into fruition.

If you haven't realized it yet, life isn't a cake walk. If it was, I probably wouldn't have written this book and half of our society wouldn't be stressed out about finding their purpose. But, the harsh truth is, life's a damn bitch sometimes and we must work for what we want for ourselves. Conscious action and effort, with time, will put you in a place of fulfillment.

So, this is one of the biggest lessons I hope you learn from this book: the importance of taking action. This is the understanding that if you want to create change, if you want to work on creating your path, and if you want to become the best version of yourself, you'll need to put your best foot forward.

Your personal growth will only continue as long as you keep stepping forward. Some days will be more difficult than others. But the sense of gratitude, appreciation, and fulfillment you'll feel on the great days will keep you pushing forward. Now is your time to take action.

2. TEACH OTHERS

Life seems much more rewarding when you bring others along for the ride. Although I wrote this book for you to learn action items you could implement in your own life, I also wrote it so you could help spread the wealth. You're a student, but you're also a teacher.

Anytime we learn things in life we hold the power to spread the wealth, or keep it all to ourselves. To an extent, I believe the correct thing to do is share that wealth. Give others your teachings so the positivity and learning can have an infinite ripple effect.

I want you to spread these words like wildfire. I want you to feel empowered by these lessons. I want that empowerment to give you the confidence that you can share what you learned here with others in hopes that you can impact their lives.

These words don't have to end here, but I need your help. I want these lessons to reach so far that I don't know how many people they've impacted. We are a team, and our goal is to encourage others to be the best version of themselves. To do that, I need you to teach others.

3. UNDERSTAND THAT YOU DESERVE EXACTLY WHAT YOU WANT IN LIFE

Lastly, above everything else, know your value and know your worth. These two aspects of life are catalysts to building up the energy and determination to chase a life worth living. You're capable of anything, as long as you tell yourself two things: 1) you can do anything you tell yourself you can and 2) you deserve this shit.

While all of these lessons and ideas hold immense power, you need to believe that you can live your dream reality for them to work to their fullest potential. If you build self-limiting beliefs by telling yourself you can't do something, these lessons will only remain as words in this book—they won't build into life changing action steps.

This book is a two-way street. I, the writer, am one way and you, the reader, are the other. For the concepts and lessons to unfold completely and be a force in your own life, you need to play an active role.

It all starts with understanding that you can live any life you want, as long as you say "I can" more times than you say "I can't." It's simple: understand that you deserve the exact life you want to live. From here, implement these action steps and lessons in the different areas you want to change and let's make this a collaborative effort.

When you need guidance, come back to this book and open the pages randomly. You'll find the lessons you need most. Things will happen as they're meant to be. That's why I've written this book with chapters that can all live alone and be read in any order. The lesson your life is craving may come forward. And, when it does, accept it, embrace it, love it, and live it.

You're taking the most important steps toward making positive changes in your life. You're stepping into your power and preparing for your journey. With each step, you'll begin to feel more motivation. I have faith in you. I believe in you. But also have faith and believe in yourself. It's the positive self-talk that will carry you the furthest. Be your own biggest cheerleader. Root for yourself both in times of hardship and success. Celebrate yourself and your conscious efforts to better your life.

Now is your time. It's your turn to chase a life you only thought you'd experience in a dream. Be a dreamer. Set lofty goals and begin the path to achieving those wild dreams.

There's no reason you should set limitations on the things you're able to achieve when *anything* is possible. Don't build a barrier between you and those wild dreams by saying "I can't." You don't have to accept what you have now. You can do whatever it is you want and live the life you deserve.

My goal with this piece of work is to inspire you to have the courage and confidence to get past the soft dirt near the beginning of your path and begin to feel more grounded as you lean against your foundation. I want to show you there's infinite potential for every single person that walks this earth, as long as you're willing to put forth the conscious effort and make the necessary positive changes.

These chapters are reminders of tools we all possess. We all need reminders, myself included, on the little things in life that help us push the needle when it comes to our personal growth. It's easy to let go and forget the seemingly insignificant aspects of life. Sometimes, all we need is a nudge in the right direction.

This book is your nudge.

THANK YOU FOR READING!

Your honest review on Amazon or through the link below would be appreciated:
www.jordantarver.com/go/ydts-review

Access free additional content below.

www.jordantarver.com/ydts-bonus-content

JORDAN TARVER'S OTHER WORK

Pursuit of Purpose:
Find Your Purpose In 30 Days
www.jordantarver.com/pursuit-of-purpose

ACKNOWLEDGEMENTS

I feel like this section of the book is usually skipped over for obvious reasons—it might not be interesting to everyone. However, I ask you to read this all the way through. I would not have been able to write this book for you without these people. They are incredibly important to my life and support me in ways I never could have imagined. I'm indebted to each and every one of them.

First I want to thank my parents, John and Karen Tarver, for always encouraging me to chase exactly what I want in life. For creating the space for me to feel empowered to make my own choices. For not giving me a predetermined path or journey, and allowing me to choose that path based on the things I hold closest to my heart. No one taught you how to parent four children, but we all can agree you did a hell of a job. You gave me a life with an amazing foundation, which was the start of me blossoming into what I've become. Thank you for being you and encouraging me to be me.

To my siblings, Evan, Lauren, and Bryan Tarver, for the constant inspiration you've all provided me throughout my life. You're all mentors to me, whether you believe it or not.

Each and every one of you are uniquely creative and ambitious with your goals and actions. Y'all are badass, and it inspires me every day. I'm grateful to consider us a unit that can't be broken. Our bond is special, remember that.

To my lovely grandma, Erni Ahlstrand, for being the beautiful soul that you are. We have always had a special bond, and I'm grateful we share that understanding. You are hands down one of the strongest individuals I know. Watching you grow into who you are today has been an incredible experience. You are very special to me. I love you, forever.

To my partner, Nicolle Rappe, for trusting me, for supporting me, for listening to my creative ideas, and for always being the collaborative piece I need for those creations. You taught me how to believe in myself and have continuously encouraged me to chase my wildest dreams, which gives me the energy to do so. Thank you for being a blessing to not only my world, but the world. You are perfectly special.

To my best friend and brother, Ryan Valasek, for cracking open the door to creativity in my life seven years ago when you let me borrow your camera until I could afford my own. You have an intelligent, dynamic, and caring soul, and you've shown me the importance of building and maintaining powerful relationships. You were my first creative inspiration, and your work still moves me to this day. Never stop creating, you have an important puzzle piece to life.

To my main support system, Drew Reynolds, Austin Maddox, Peter Engfelt, Tommy Mulder, and Reese Moulton, for being the best team I could ask for. You all have provided me with a group of incredibly successful individuals who motivate each other to own their life. Your work ethic inspires me, and the support you give to my work is uncanny.

To my adventure mate and one of my closest friends, Troy Rupp, for sharing a passion for the outdoors, camping, photography, and all things creative. You were one of my earliest inspirations in photography, and I'm grateful we've always shared the same enthusiasm for life on the go. I've always appreciated not only your work but the support you give mine. I hope you never stop shooting, never stop filming, and never stop creating. Your art is special, don't let it go.

To my partner's parents, Lorrie and Grey Rappe, for always being there to listen to my wild ideas and not telling me I'm crazy but telling me to go for it. The support you give me both in my personal and professional life is hard to come by. From showing up on release days to getting me back up to health when I need it most, it all adds up. I am forever grateful for our relationship.

To my brother from another mother, Jake Rappe, for being an honest and supportive friend that's more than willing to help me along my journey of other creative ventures. I value our relationship more than you know, and I see you as a brother. Keep chasing your dreams, you have no limit. You are talent.

To the guy I can always count on, Tyler Henry, for coming into my life and career at a crucial turning point. You've supported my ideas, backed my creativity, and given me another person in my corner. You make yourself available to others, including myself, even when we all know how much you're working on yourself. That's a unique quality and one I never take for granted.

To my fellow outdoor enthusiast, Brian Lee, for being the friend I can always count on for a meaningful conversation when I need it most. Whether that conversation is out on a trail or in the morning when I was writing this book, it's always a damn good one. You are nothing but genuine. Thank you for being a support system any artist needs and cultivating the artist within yourself. Don't hold back, your art impacts the world.

To my dear friend, Blake Drewette, for always being someone I can rely on. I appreciate your love for art and the support you give to me. Our relationship is a special one, and I'm happy we've found a connection over music and self-expression. There are a lot of years in front of us, let's keep doing what we do best.

To my east coast brother, Jesse Cyrulnik, for giving me so much of your time to help me with new creative passions. I never thought a remote job would introduce me to a friendship I value as much as ours. Your creativity is impeccable and there is a lot of creative success in your future. Keeping following your heart, it's leading you in the right direction.

To my editor, Cindy Draughon, for taking this book to the next level and helping find more opportunities to deliver my message. While I felt like I was stuck in an edit and feedback loop forever, every minute was well worth it because of the quality of your work. Connecting with you felt more than right, and I knew you were the missing piece to the words on these pages. I appreciate your conscious effort when it came to looking for ways to elevate my writing.

To every person that's ever told me they believed in me, you've been there for me for when I couldn't. You've supported my work, my art, and my creativity through and through. Every time you've praised my work or been there on a release day, I've gone home with the power to continue creating. That support has fueled so much in my life, and I don't know where I would be without it. I respect your kind words of appreciation and love, and I'm genuinely happy to have you on this journey forever. Thank you.

And finally, to you for taking the time to read this book. Thank you for taking it upon yourself to want to create positive change in your own life. I'm excited to see where your journey of self-discovery will take you. Be prepared to arrive at somewhere amazing.

ABOUT THE AUTHOR

Jordan Tarver is a passionate outdoorsman and adventurer. As an introspective writer, photographer, and author, you'll find that the majority of his work focuses around one overarching theme: how to live a more meaningful life. His work is designed to investigate the depth of life beyond materialism, and be a toolkit for self-discovery and becoming the best version of yourself.

Jordan's first two books, *Moment* and *You Deserve This Shit*, are the result of several years of tireless creative self-work. He strives to turn his experiences into teaching moments for others because he believes everyone deserves to live a life fueled with purpose. Those teaching moments are there to help guide others in a positive direction.

In addition to being an author, Jordan also focuses a lot of his time in the outdoor community. He's a profound adventure photographer and writes long-form adventure essays to explore the true meaning of the outdoors and its relationship to people. In 2018, he joined the van life community and self-converted a campervan. His van gives him access to explore different regions of the country and share experiences with his surrounding community.

You can support Jordan's work on Instagram, he is @jordantarver, or visit his website: www.jordantarver.com

Made in United States
Orlando, FL
13 December 2023